The Mirror that SPEAKS BACK

The Bible Reading Fellowship
15 The Chambers, Vineyard
Abingdon OX14 3FE
brf.org.uk

The Bible Reading Fellowship (BRF) is a Registered Charity (233280)

ISBN 978 0 85746 635 8
First published 2018
10 9 8 7 6 5 4 3 2 1 0

Cover image © Thinkstock, typography by Rebecca J Hall

Acknowledgements
Unless otherwise stated, scripture quotations are taken from The Holy Bible, New International Version (Anglicised edition) copyright © 1979, 1984, 2011 by Biblica. Used by permission of Hodder & Stoughton Publishers, an Hachette UK company. All rights reserved. 'NIV' is a registered trademark of Biblica. UK trademark number 1448790

Scripture quotations taken from The Message (MSG), copyright © 1993, 1994, 1995, 1996, 2000, 2001, 2002 by Eugene H. Peterson. Used by permission of NavPress. All rights reserved. Represented by Tyndale House Publishers, Inc.

Scripture quotations taken from the Amplified® Bible (AMP), copyright © 2015 by The Lockman Foundation. Used by permission. www.lockman.org.

Scripture quotations taken from the Holy Bible, English Standard Version (ESV), published by HarperCollins Publishers, © 2001 Crossway Bibles, a division of Good News Publishers. Used by permission. All rights reserved.

Scripture quotations taken from The Living Bible (TLB) copyright © 1971 by Tyndale House Foundation. Used by permission of Tyndale House Publishers Inc., Carol Stream, Illinois 60188. All rights reserved. The Living Bible, TLB, and the The Living Bible logo are registered trademarks of Tyndale House Publishers.

Every effort has been made to trace and contact copyright owners for material used in this resource. We apologise for any inadvertent omissions or errors, and would ask those concerned to contact us so that full acknowledgement can be made in the future.

A catalogue record for this book is available from the British Library

Printed and bound by CPI Group (UK) Ltd, Croydon CR0 4YY

The Mirror that SPEAKS BACK

Looking at, listening to and
reflecting your worth in Jesus

Anne Le Tissier

BRF

Contents

Foreword by Amy Boucher Pye 7

Introduction 9

Part I What's it all about? Addressing the problem

1 Mirror messages 19
2 'Apart from you' 28
3 'Do the Book. Do it!' 37

Part II The mirror messages

4 Mirror, mirror, on the wall 49
5 Restoring my true identity 59
6 God's purpose despite my health 69
7 The endless feed 79
8 A subjective subject 90
9 Restoring my first love 100
10 A twist in the tale 110
11 Inflated, deflated or Jesus-motivated 120

Part III Moving on

12 A cautionary tale 131
13 Learning to be content 141
14 Beyond this book 150

Notes 158

Foreword

As I stood in the doorway, I felt like an invisible wall prohibited me from entering. I was welcome to join the reception at the publishing company where I worked, but I felt intimidated, not least because I didn't know many of the people from the other departments. As I watched them chatting and mingling, I felt stuck, unable to enter. After a few minutes, a colleague came along and said, 'Aren't you going in?' I felt a rush of shame and said, 'No, I guess not,' and dashed back to the safety of my office.

Finding our sense of self and finding ourselves in God can be a long journey – the story I share above happened when I was in my early 30s, after I had grappled with issues of identity and self-acceptance for years. Although I was no longer stuck in a pattern of self-hatred like I had been before, I still experienced moments when the voices of not being enough – or being too much – would crowd out the loving voice of God.

Such negative messages bombard us continually, whether through social media, advertising, peers or even ourselves. We feel we don't measure up and never will. We feel too fat, too thin, too loud, too quiet, too much, too little, too (insert your adjective here). As we listen to those words whispered to us, or shouted at us, we start to believe them.

But, as Anne Le Tissier writes so wisely and so well, we don't need to be beholden to these lies and false proclamations. We can turn to the truth of God's word and his still, small voice, in which he affirms the truth of who we are in him.

Anne shares deeply of herself and her story as she points us to our solid foundation in God. Because he created and formed us in his image, we need not be ashamed. We are sinful, but God through his Son Jesus redeems us. Anne describes the journey she has travelled through shame, negative self-talk, an eating disorder and suffering abuse. But God rescued her, and she learned to replace the unholy habits with regular practices that led to life and growth.

Anne is a lovely companion in *The Mirror That Speaks Back* to walk alongside us as we examine some hard but necessary things. She directs us to look to God for his truth and his ways, where we will find hope and healing. Be encouraged during this journey, knowing that God is in the transforming business.

Amy Boucher Pye, writer, speaker and author of
***The Living Cross* (BRF, 2016)**

Introduction

The thief comes only to steal and kill and destroy; I have come that they may have life, and have it to the full.
JOHN 10:10

I came that they may have *and* enjoy life, and have it in abundance [to the full, till it overflows].
JOHN 10:10 (AMP)

My story

My husband and I were walking a stretch of the beautiful Cotswold Way when we spotted it: a lamb squirming in a desperate fight to free its trapped head, stuck between entwined branches which hung low to the ground from an ancient, twisted tree.

Its mother stood nearby, bleating comfort but unable to help.

With gentle voices and slow steps, we drew alongside two terrified, bulging brown eyes. I placed my arms around its neck, still speaking in soft tones, and as my husband forced two branches apart, I guided the lamb backwards out of its snare.

'I think we should stop for a cuppa,' I suggested with a grin, pulling a flask from my rucksack, as the lamb skittered away with its mum.

I was once like that lamb: alive, yes, but unable to live life as God intended.

This was when my self-image plummeted during my late teens and early 20s. I was driven to please significant others, failing exams I should never have sat, and despairing at the impossible pressure to clone the 'ideal' body shape idolised in adverts and the media. I was cheated on repeatedly by one boyfriend, endured an abusive relationship with another, and by the time I did get engaged I was still overcoming an eating disorder.

I believed in my head in God's love, but low self-image held me back from experiencing its fullness at the core of my inner being. I was discontent with who I was and lacked confidence to pursue everything that God had made me to be.

Jesus promised 'life… to the full' (John 10:10), but I knew I wasn't receiving it in the way the Bible suggested. And if not for being offered a choice to engage with the power of God's word, I would still be like that lamb – alive but held back from living out the promise for myself.

What this book is *not* intended to be

This book is not just intended for women with eating disorders. The consequences of low self-image are many and varied. But whatever their nature, their presence suggests we are not experiencing God's love to the full measure and will likely struggle to pursue and fulfil our God-given potential.

Nor is this book competing with authoritative, educational books on self-image. I am not trained to write such a book – nor was I asked to! – but I am qualified to draw on my personal experience with self-esteem, self-worth and body-image issues, alongside my knowledge of God's love and the life-transforming healing effect of proactively engaging with his word.

This book is more of a living, breathing, instructive story of how God shifted the axis of my life from a negative self-image to a healthy identity and understanding of my worth in him; and how he can change your life too.

But here I must include a word of caution, for those of you whose low self-image has already contributed to mental or physical health problems.

God has healed, and continues to heal, many individuals of sickness, sometimes by a powerful encounter with the Holy Spirit and sometimes in conjunction with medication. This book is not intended to replace professional treatment; I am not a qualified medic or certified counsellor. Cognitive behavioural therapy (CBT)[1], counselling and/or prescribed medication may be required if your health and life are already at risk (through clinical depression, alcohol or drug addiction, self-harm or eating disorders).

If you think you fall into that category then do still read this book, but be encouraged, right now, to seek the medical help you need as well.

We do not live in a perfect world – that still waits for us in heaven – and it is often through the God-given expertise of professionals that we are helped to live meaningful lives, even within our broken environment.

Why *The Mirror That Speaks Back*?

> *When a girl doesn't feel good about herself, she isn't reaching her full potential.*
> Dove Self-Esteem Project[2]

Modern Western culture conveys, usually through images in the media, a message of happiness, contentment and fulfilment that all too often depends on having the 'ideal' face or body shape, wearing the latest fashion or achieving certain benchmarks of success, including top exam grades, an exciting gap-year experience, a high-flying career, promotion, marriage and giving birth.

These are the alternative 'mirrors' which society offers to measure worth, but when we look at and listen to them we begin to hear a repeated message: I'm not good enough; I'm not attractive enough; I don't have enough.

In short, we're just never *enough*.

If we start to believe, even subconsciously, that these distortions are the ideals we should conform or aspire to, they have the power to undermine our self-image and the potential to harm our physical, mental or spiritual health.

And Christian women are not immune to the problem.

Many Christian women have shared with me that while they believe their faith should protect them from feeling unloved, insecure, inadequate or ugly, in reality their self-image can be as low as that of their non-Christian friends. They believe God's word is true, but they struggle to let it transform their response to peer and cultural pressure. So negative messages or demanding expectations undermine their pursuit and experience of the contented, fulfilling and influential life God intends for them.

Ellen (not her real name) suffers from bulimia, an eating disorder that has grown out of her negative body image. She writes:

I feel so disappointed in myself for feeling so close to God, but still letting this issue bother me. It seems that, no matter how much I know, the 'switch just isn't flicking'. The Bible verses are encouraging but no matter how much information goes in, I just don't feel it.

I know from experience that merely being handed scripture is unlikely to provide a miraculous cure for anxiety, self-hatred, feeling unworthy or any other debilitating lack of well-being. That is why I will share my own story of how God inspired me to root myself deeper into his love and proactively engage with his word; that is, to trust it and walk it out, rather than just to be familiar with it. For this was the powerful remedy for my low self-image, as well as a protective barrier against further onslaught.

In the same way that I approached that lamb, and used the strength of my husband's arms to help it find freedom, I believe that God wants me to come alongside you, place an arm around your shoulders and help you to engage with the power of his truth that sets you free – to release you from the snares that stop you living in and experiencing the fullness of life that he intended.

I am going to quote, pray and dig into scripture, but I hope you will allow me to walk *with* you and speak *with* you – to journey with you through this part of your life – and not just spurt out truth at you from a distance.

I will also encourage you to talk with God and, in turn, I trust that his living power will do his work of healing in and through you.

The apostle Paul had 'learned' to be content in all circumstances (Philippians 4:12). If we can learn how to be content, we can today experience Christ's promise of an abundant life, instead of it being diluted or distorted by self-image issues. We can learn to be content with ourselves, today, rather than suffering years – even decades – of needless anxiety, unfulfilled potential, problematic relationships or chasing meaningless goals, and can avoid the downward spiral into dangerous health problems.

Life will still be tough at times. Christ's promise of life to the full and the contentment in God that Paul writes about do not mean immunity from problems. But they do speak of God's empowering to overcome whatever undermines our inward security and limits our experience of his love.

So I pray that, by the time you close this book, you too will be well on the way to learning contentment – with how you look, with what you can do (as well as what you can't), with your relationships, with your health and, most of all, with God.

Your story

As part of my research for this book I devised a questionnaire. Many young women (aged 16–28) responded by email, via post or through group discussions, and I am extremely grateful for their honesty and vulnerability. The culture has changed since I was their age, and while some of the negative pressures are similar, many are new or different. Here are two short examples from Amelia (not her real name):

What makes you feel inadequate, a failure, unlovable or ugly?
When someone makes negative comments about my weight or appearance.

Every generation has its 'giants to slay'. What are yours?
My worries for getting a job in the future, and body-image concerns.

I thank these women again, for without exception every respondent offered invaluable authenticity to this book. You will read their responses as quotes under pseudonyms,[3] but you will also have the opportunity to answer some of the questions yourself, along with others included just for this book.

Pause to respond to God

The Mirror That Speaks Back is divided into three parts:

1 Introducing the problem and how to deal with it.
2 A look at some cultural 'mirrors' that can undermine self-image, and how to overcome them.
3 Some concluding warnings and tips to help you move on.

Every chapter, however, encourages you to pause before turning the page, to pray through or worship God with your response to what you are learning.

I have offered suggestions to help you, but do give time for the Holy Spirit to breathe life into your heart, then respond in whatever way he leads you. For now, I'd love to pray for you myself:

Jesus, please empower your truth in this young woman's heart. Release her from whatever is restricting her experience of the fullness of life you promised. May she turn the final page at peace with who she is in you and inspired to pursue all that you created her to be. Amen

Role models who inspire for reasons other than their appearance

With the exception of two chapters with footnotes, each chapter concludes with a response from my final research question:

Is there an older woman (Christian or not) who inspires you, but NOT because of her looks? Who is she, and what is it about her that influences you for the good?

Here is the first:

> *My role models are women who inspire me to nurture and grow*
> *the qualities I see in their lives, like patience.*
> Yasmin

I wonder who inspires you to nurture such qualities.

What's it all about?

Addressing the problem

1

Mirror messages

Why the need for this book?

**You weren't born thinking, 'I'm not good enough.'
Someone or something made you feel that way, perhaps a
long time ago.**
Chris Williams[4]

My story

Home for me while growing up was mum, dad, elder sister and
brother, plus various cats, hamsters, fish, rabbits and budgerigars,
arriving and departing over the years. It was a loving, generous and
supportive place of nurture and growth.

My sister could be rebellious at times; I'd bury my head under pillows
to muffle the yelling and banging of doors. Perhaps that is why I am
still disturbed by loud noise or raised voices. But she and I have
always been close. She never failed to look out for me and I always
looked up to her. I was proud of her (and still am). She was my big
sis: fun, intelligent and an excellent swimmer, diver and trampolinist.
She was also my idol – she seemed to know what life was all about
and could answer my girlish questions.

I only grew close to my brother, however, through my teens and adulthood. During childhood, he would bully me, threaten me and shoot his rubber-tipped arrows or pellet gun at me. Although these were no different from other sibling pranks, the childhood fears they created fed into my anxious nature.

Apart from that, it was not until my mid-to-late teens that certain negative messages undermined my well-being:

- Cloakroom jokes about pancakes and bra size became all too shaming – I was a late developer and have always been petite.
- The disappointment in my father's face when I failed my A levels – having foolishly studied subjects I was weaker at to please him – then applied for a job in a merchant bank rather than to study at university.
- The message that I wasn't good enough each time my first boyfriend was unfaithful.
- The mental, verbal, emotional and occasional physical abuse that I endured in the next relationship.

So around the time I was your age (if you still call yourself a young woman), my sense of self-worth and self-esteem, not least in terms of my body image, was reeling from failure and inadequacy.

That said, it certainly wasn't all doom and gloom:

- Mum has been a constant refuge and support.
- I came to faith when I was 15, despite my unchurched upbringing.
- My dad's disappointment was soon overcome when I sped up the ranks of promotion.
- I developed new and positive relationships.
- Timid me took off alone on a round-the-world ticket, including a stint with Youth with a Mission (YWAM) New Zealand.[5]
- I married the best man God could have chosen for me, and cherish the gift of my daughter.

I would like to say these positives brought healing to my low self-image. In many ways they played a part, but they were never enough. Ultimately, I still had to choose to hear God speaking to me and to hold on to his messages, digest them and infuse my battered inner life with wholeness – unconditional acceptance, intimate understanding, contentment, purpose and peace. I had to stop conforming to cultural pressures and expectations, and allow my priorities to be transformed by God.

Mirror messages

I hate looking in mirrors, and have them covered up at home. Looking in a mirror physically makes me feel sick. I hate my body. I hate everything about me.
Amy

This upsetting quote reminds us of why we look into mirrors, which is, of course, to see the image reflected back – to check our hair, make-up or outfit or to search for that lost thigh gap!

But here is the problem.

Amy's hatred of glass mirrors stems from the alternative 'mirrors' society offers to gauge how well she matches up to its ideal. And she's certainly not alone.

Daily, if not hourly, we are assailed, inundated and at times overwhelmed by hundreds of mirror images and messages, reflections that try to imprint their own pattern on our thinking – their blueprint of what is necessary to feel good about life. Other people's opinions, professional photo shoots, social media, exam-grade benchmarks and the fashion, beauty and diet industries: these are just a few of the mirrors that reflect back how they think we should look or be or do or behave, and how far we fall short. They are mirrors that convey and communicate who and what we are in *society's* opinion.

But no mirror is perfect. Flaws in manufactured glass mirrors distort reflections: warped glass ripples the image (as in the hall of mirrors at a 'funfair'), while any irregularities in the coating applied to the back can make us appear fatter, thinner, brighter or duller than we actually are.

Society's mirrors are just as flawed. These mirrors misrepresent God's truth, so when we prioritise time, effort or money in trying to conform to their distorted ideals, they sow seeds of discontent in our souls. That's why advertising is a multibillion-dollar industry, because repeated messages affect what we think and feel, and consequently what we do. One moment, we are lounging on the sofa feeling content. Then an advert appears and suddenly we feel hungry, dowdy or old – we raid the fridge, arrange a shopping trip or make a Botox appointment. Repetitive messages have the power to cut deep into our self-image and well-being.

Only Jesus offers a mirror that reflects a faultless image of who we were made to be. For Jesus himself is the 'radiance of God's glory and the exact representation of his being' (Hebrews 1:3), and we have been predestined to be conformed into that image, to grow into his likeness, just as God originally created us to be (Romans 8:29; Genesis 1:26).

> *Do not conform to the pattern of this world, but be transformed*
> *by the renewing of your mind.*
> ROMANS 12:2

This is something we will learn to do in practical and meaningful ways throughout this book, inviting the imprint of God's image and truth to transform our thoughts and renew our identity in Jesus.

Your story

Self-criticism, or thinking about what people think, can be a mind battle. When you focus on it you get beaten up! But it helps to come back to the value Jesus has for you.
Natalie

You might like to grab a notebook to journal your responses; it could prove useful to recall them as you keep working through this book.

Consider the following words:

Inadequate
Failure
Unlovable
Imposter
Shallow
Silly
Foolish
Ugly

- Can you relate to any of them?
- What other labels do you pin to yourself?
- Who or what makes you feel that way?

Who or what makes you feel under pressure to do something or to conform to an ideal? If nothing comes to mind, consider these examples:

- friends' comments
- lack of care or encouragement from family
- your body
- your weight
- pressure to conform to fashion or make-up ideals
- lack of money to buy the clothes or make-up you feel expected to wear

- images in magazines, on the internet or on TV
- your Christian beliefs
- your level of intellect or general knowledge
- your capability, skills or talents
- social media

How do any negative feelings:

- affect your mental and physical health, or your focus on Jesus?
- stop you doing or saying something?
- put pressure on you to do or say something?
- hinder you from living the life you believe God intended for you?

Taking it further

Remember that the key to the discipline of study is not reading many books but experiencing what we do read.
Richard J. Foster[6]

I am going to share some of my story throughout this book, because I want to be real with you; I want to open my heart to you, so that you can feel safe to open your heart to God. As we journey together, I will take your chin in my hand, as it were, and turn your face away from the world's Vegas-like mirrors, to gaze into the mirror of Jesus – to see, and grow to love and yearn for, the image and likeness our Father longs for each of us to aspire to.

But I need your help, as I can't do all of this for you!

Be honest with yourself and with God. *Really* honest. This means you will probably need time to pause in each chapter, in order to reflect on the teaching and questions, rather than hastily turning the page, and mull over what Jesus is saying to *you* through the messages from his word that we will unpack together; time to think practically how you might 'take further action' with the ideas proposed.

Pause to respond to God

Pause for a while, to love and be loved in worship and prayer by your creator, Father and very best friend – your only true source of complete contentment and well-being.

If you are struggling to believe Jesus can truly bring freedom from the pressures on you to conform to the world, then talk to him about it now. Be open about any doubts you have that he wants to heal your low self-esteem or body image.

Talk to him about your responses to the questions above. Be honest, and just talk to him. This prayer (inspired by Mark 9:24b) might help you to start:

Jesus, I do believe in my head. I believe you are all-powerful to free me from the world's mirror images and messages. But I also fear how that will fit with my family's expectations, my friends' opinions, and my relationship and employment prospects. Help me to believe in my heart and not just my head that you really are my true source of contentment and self-worth, and hold my hand as we walk this journey together to full healing and release.

Role models who inspire for reasons other than their appearance

I am inspired by a close friend who is only my senior by about two months! She's become a bit of a feminist and she challenges a lot of the stereotypical body-image standards for women. For example, why is it that girls' legs are seen as better looking and more attractive when they are shaved? It's stuff that I would never have thought about, and then she goes further and acts on her beliefs, and isn't afraid to make a statement or talk about her opinions.

Molly

Footnote: some definitions

My will to continue writing this book almost drowned in a tidal wave of definitions and explanations. Copious research offered shifting opinions over what these terms mean, but eventually I re-emerged, clutching at repeated core themes.

So do read these descriptions, but please don't get bogged down in them. The terms in daily life are often used synonymously, so I feel sure we can continue with a simple overview.

Self-esteem – Confidence in and respect for our personality, abilities and appearance; an assurance that we have a positive and meaningful contribution to make to life and relationships.

Low self-esteem may involve feelings or beliefs of being inadequate, incompetent, incapable, worthless, unworthy, insignificant, unimportant, a failure, low in confidence, unlovable and unlikeable. It can drive self-hate, guilt, fear and/or perfectionism. It can stop us from fulfilling our God-given potential or from living the life God created for us to live. It can trigger addictions and mental disorders and undermine our relationships with others, not least with God.

Body image – How we perceive our physical body, and how we assume others perceive it; the level of satisfaction and confidence we have with our body; the disparity between our perception of what the ideal body should look like and what our body actually looks like.

The outcomes of a low body image dovetail with those above for low self-esteem, and also include depression, eating disorders, risky behaviour (such as unsafe sex), self-harming and cosmetic surgery. It can also lead to withdrawal from social activities, playing sports or intimacy with our partner; reluctance to wear certain clothing; and fear of being the centre of attention, performing with music and drama, or fulfilling an upfront leadership or presenter role.

Self-worth – Our sense of personal value or worth; a belief that we deserve a place in the world.

A healthy self-worth accepts our inherent value, but if we measure our worth by comparing ourselves to others, there will always be 'others' who seem to do 'it' better than us.

Lack of or low self-worth can damage our relationships and our mental, emotional, physical and spiritual well-being. It undermines our dreams and accomplishments and, in turn, causes us to doubt we can give any significant value to life.

Self-image – Includes a number of impressions that we build up about ourselves over time. Some say it is synonymous with self-esteem or self-worth; others disagree. But it does involve how we perceive ourselves, which is often influenced by how we think others perceive us, what we had hoped to do or feel compared to what actually happened, or both.

An unrealistic positive self-image can encourage apathy or arrogance; a realistic one will build contentment and confidence. An unrealistic negative self-image can cause us to suffer the many consequences already described above, but a realistic one will inspire change or motivate a harder work ethic.

Self-acceptance – The realistic but unconditional attitude we adopt about ourselves at any particular moment, regardless of how well we are fulfilling expectations, dreams or goals. We may 'fail' to reach that goal or expectation, but accept that this is who we are today, with potential for growth or change.

A lack of self-acceptance, however, may in turn affect our self-esteem, self-worth or body image.

2

'Apart from you'

It all starts with him

Whatever has got your attention has got you.
Anon.

My story

Perhaps it was the barking dogs in the street below that woke me, or the high-pitched horns or traders' shouts, but before I had opened my eyes I could smell it: the sour, spicy, earthy, fumy, sewer-and-sweat-type pungency, infusing the heat and humidity of 6.00 am Bombay.

My palm scanned skin for fresh bedbug bites, pausing to caress my cramping belly.

I opened my eyes.

No gecko looking down at me from the peeling paintwork today; perhaps it had joined the cockroaches in the bathroom.

Four other women slept on as I sat up on my bunk bed, my heart tugging for home and family 4,588 miles away. My niece would be celebrating her second birthday – without Aunty Anne.

Heavy-hearted, I flipped my Bible open to its bookmarked page and started reading Psalm 16. But I only read as far as verse 2: 'You are my Lord; apart from you I have no good thing.'

I read it again. And again. Then I glanced up, gazing out at nothing through the paneless wire-meshed window.

You are my Lord…

Yes, I could say that Jesus was my Lord. I believed in him for forgiveness and eternal life. I had left a promising career and a man I had loved, because he didn't share my faith, to cross the world, train with YWAM and share God's love among India's poor.

My faith had certainly deepened, both in theory (from uninterrupted hours alone in the word, then the fabulous discipleship training) and in practice (when my luggage went missing for three weeks between Thailand and Australia, and then through timidly approaching strangers on India's streets to talk about God). Of course, I wasn't perfect; there was so much more I needed to change, do and surrender, but I felt I could say that Jesus was my Lord.

…apart from you I have no good thing.

It was the last part of verse 2 that tripped me up, my homesickness betraying me. Desperate for time with family, safe drinking water and cool, clean sheets, I had to admit that apart from Jesus I had lots of good things: people I loved, possessions, work and a life to return to, beyond the scope of travel and short-term mission.

So the challenge of this verse glared brightly beneath the Indian sun, as the Holy Spirit ignited a yearning to be like the writer of Psalm 16.

I wanted Jesus to know this prayer to be real for me, too: that in comparison with everything and everyone else in my life, I could honestly say he was the only good thing; that despite the gift of many loving relationships and material blessings, Jesus would always have and be my first love.

But there was a chasm between where I wanted to be and where I was on that day.

Looking into the flawless mirror

'Apart from me, Anne,' Jesus says, 'there is absolutely nothing that can even begin to compare with my unrelenting love, my dependability and credibility, my understanding and insight, my promises that I will never fail to keep, my boundless presence and immortality. I am the only one who can truly say I will *never* leave you.'

Let's think on that for a moment.

We are bombarded with endless mirror images and messages, pushing us to conform with, or strive to match up to, their distorted expectations:

- This is how you should look if you want to be beautiful.
- This is the image you should adopt if you want to be accepted, respected and popular.
- This is the success you should achieve if you want a fulfilled life.
- This is the book, blog or article that will teach you the best way to live.
- This is the type of relationship that will satisfy your need to be loved, cherished and intimately understood.

And dare I add:

- This is the type of Christian you should be, to be empowered by God.

Now reread those words of Jesus above, inserting your name in place of mine. Do you sense any tension? Perhaps it sounds like this:

Yes, I believe in my head what you are saying, Lord, but if I'm honest, my longings and ambitions are still fuelled by the value and meaning in life that other mirrors reflect. In this moment, Lord, what you are saying sounds great! But in the reality of day-to-day life, my need to be accepted among my friends, my longing for a partner to make me feel special, my striving for some kind of purpose in life and my sense of inadequacy if I don't look like so-and-so, do what they do or achieve their success, distract me from what I know about you in my head.

Whether or not that sounds familiar, there are times we may not be aware of this internal dialogue, as the subliminal mirror messages lure a subconscious response from our hearts. All we know is that we worry too much about how we look, how we can be good enough or what other people think of us. And if someone hasn't done so already, we slap labels on ourselves, controlling how we feel about life.

I spent three weeks reflecting on Psalm 16:2, before moving on to verse 3, and have aspired to it ever since. Through these few but profound words, God helped me to understand that until he was the undisputed first love of my heart, and not just one love of many, I would continue to suffer from a lack of self-worth, low self-esteem and shattered body image and quite possibly get worse, despite my professed faith. I learned that to break free from my self-imposed labels, or the expectations of others that dictated and distorted my self-image, I needed to find out who I was *in him* – something I now put to you.

We need to 'find ourselves' in his love; revel in it, root and establish ourselves in it, and grow out from it so that we don't just know about it in our head, but experience it deep in our soul, that we 'may be filled to the measure of all the fullness of God' (Ephesians 3:19).

Because Paul lived life from the place of being 'found' in Jesus, he was content with life, no matter his circumstances. Like David in Psalm 16:2, Paul considered all else as rubbish compared with *knowing* Jesus (Philippians 3:8–10). His letters suggest he cherished his friendships and work, but compared with them knowing Jesus was so very much better.

So let's find the way to being in that place too: where set against the daily experience of being loved by, and loving, God, all else is comparatively 'rubbish' or 'no good' – where the ideals of beauty, definitions of success and aspirations to be accepted by others won't even come close to feeding the essence of who we are.

Fostering a desire for our first love

> *I know that Jesus' love should be enough to overcome my feelings of lack of worth, and I do pray, but I don't feel the worth that I might from the words or a hug from a friend. It's hard to sense his love because he's not visible or audible, but I know I need it to overcome my self-worth issues.*
> Jen

Paul says, 'It's in Christ that we find out who we are and what we are living for' (Ephesians 1:11, MSG). So how do we make that a reality?

As a first step, remember the following.

It takes more than one prayer to develop a deeper relationship

It takes time to get to know and fully appreciate someone. So let's start by making space in our day to *know* God more fully, just as we make time to be with a person we want to befriend or are attracted to.

But let's not leave our awareness of him back in that place of pause. Much of our engaging with God will come from knowing him with us right through the day, choosing to be aware of his presence until he becomes our natural focus.

There is a choice to be made

I'm going to talk about choice rather a lot in this book. But if we want the value we have in God to impact our sense of peace, worth, purpose and contentment, we will need to choose to look at and listen to the mirror images and messages that he offers in his word. Regularly.

Imagine how many times each day you check your hair or look at your social-media feed. Any guesses? But how often do you check a negative thought (or proud response) against what God is saying?

Knowing God's word in our head is one thing, but when we root and establish our whole being in it we start feeling secure. At first it may need to be a conscious choice, but in time it will become a natural habit.

Your story

Above all else, guard your affections. For they influence everything else in your life.
PROVERBS 4:23 (TLB)

- Who or what do you turn to first, for comfort, reassurance, guidance and to make you feel better about your life?
- How have they helped you permanently?
- How have they let you down?

'For where your treasure is, there your heart will be also.'
MATTHEW 6:21

- Who or what do you think is the treasure of your heart? To help you answer, consider what you think about most, how you fill your free time, what you spend your money on and what excites or energises you. Is it possible that some of these things may be treasures competing for God's first love in your heart?
- Do you struggle to believe or receive God's love for you? If so, can you identify why? The suggestion in 'Taking it further', below, will help you begin to heal that distorted message.

[You are] predestined to be conformed to the image of [Jesus].
ROMANS 8:29

- Think about how Jesus lived his life from what you've seen and heard about in the Gospels.
- What does that image look like to you?
- Spend time reflecting on any characteristics that particularly inspire or reassure you.

Taking it further

My faith and relationship with Jesus help me, because I know he loves me despite it all.
Penny

If you don't do so already, in your Bible start to highlight or underline words that describe how God sees you, feels about you, values you, accepts you, loves you, rejoices over you, desires you and is with you, and the many other images and messages that reflect the depth of his love for you.

Then, when you need a message of truth to counter a distorted one, you can flick through your Bible and see them immediately. (This is one of the advantages of using a hard-copy Bible, even if you also use one on your phone.)

This exercise will take you as long as it takes to read the entire Bible, but here are some examples to get you going (you will find more in later chapters too): Psalm 3:3; 5:12; 9:9–10; 23; 86:5; 139; 145; Isaiah 41:10; 43:1; Jeremiah 31:3; Zephaniah 3:17; Matthew 28:20; John 1:12; 14:23; 15:15; Romans 8:17; 1 Corinthians 6:19; Ephesians 3:18; Hebrews 13:5–6; 1 Peter 5:7; 1 John 2:12.

These words convey *God's* image of *you*; they are God's way of reflecting back to you who you are in him. How does that make you feel?

Pause to respond to God

For many years I've been using a prayer I adapted from Ephesians 1:17–18. It is more than words; it comes from my heart's longing for an ever-deepening union with Jesus – a longing I hope you share, so that you can pray this prayer from your heart too:

Jesus, I'm asking, and I am going to keep on asking, that you will fill me again with your Spirit of wisdom and revelation, to give me a deeper awareness and experience of you. I really do want to know you more. Please open the spiritual eyes of my heart ever wider, so that I may understand, appreciate and experience what it is to have my life enriched with your heavenly presence today. Amen

You could also make time to worship God with songs that reflect this divine relationship. Take a look on YouTube for appropriate songs. Sing along or just soak in the music and lyrics. Depending on your taste in music, you may like to start with 'Found' by Hillsong or 'Good Good Father' by Chris Tomlin.

Role models who inspire for reasons other than their appearance

None of the women who inspire me are inspirational because of their looks. One of my favourite Christian speakers is Miriam Swaffield; although she is pretty, it's her faith and mission I respect.

Alice

3

'Do the Book. Do it!'

The key to transformation

When you read the Word, say, 'God speak to me and whatever you tell me, I will do it'… Do the Book. Do it!
Brother Andrew[7]

My story

They had a way of making me feel small, inadequate. Time after time, their barbed comments found their target with sniper-like precision, leaving me floundering in a wake of inability and shame.

At first, I used to smile sweetly, waiting until I could excuse myself to shed private tears in the bathroom. But the scar tissue hardened with the passing of years. My heart toughened, learning to give as good as it got, reacting unkindly, often with spite, then grovelling at Jesus' feet to forgive my loveless behaviour, and seeking where possible to put things right for offending the offender.

It was an exhausting emotional tussle: the fear of the next onslaught, the intensity of the battle, the guilt of the aftermath. No matter how determined I was to be 'godlier' in future, my resilience to the jibes weakened with each painful encounter.

One day they came to visit, not just for lunch, not just for a few hours, but for seven whole days. I prayed well in advance. I imagined familiar scenarios and planned gracious replies. I prayed some more, preparing myself to be the kind of person Jesus wanted me to be.

The doorbell rang in time to share a light lunch, but by the time I stood up to clear away soup bowls, I had already let myself and God down badly.

The following day, in the early hour that is silent and still, I asked – yet again – for forgiveness, then opened my hands. 'Fill me with your love, Lord. Mine just isn't enough. Work in me your humility and compassion,' I prayed.

I waited awhile, then found myself asking for wisdom, to help me move with grace into the rest of the day. Immediately, two verses came to mind:

> 'In repentance and rest is your salvation, in quietness and trust is your strength…'
> ISAIAH 30:15

> The fruit of that righteousness will be peace; its effect will be quietness and confidence for ever.
> ISAIAH 32:17

My efforts to stop my snappy retorts had proved disastrous, but I sensed Jesus urging me to take my eyes off the offender and focus my attention on not offending *him*. Living out of that perspective, I would find a quiet rest for my soul, as I trusted him to deal with the offender in his own time and way.

For the next six days, I repeated these verses hourly and whenever the conversation turned against me. They stilled my tongue. They focused my mind on Christ's righteousness, rather than my own or others' imperfections. They filled my heart with loving consideration for those he also loved, and so I experienced the promised fruit – the product and outworking of responding proactively to these truths: peace.

The fruit of allowing *Christ's* righteousness to work its transforming effect was peace with myself, peace with the offender and peace with God.

Both verses took deeper root throughout the visit, to the extent that I experienced a new confidence in who I was in God – a quiet but empowering security that no one else's words or behaviour could undermine.

Putting it into practice

> *If you are experiencing God in his word, you will have strength and wisdom, but make no mistake, you will also have stability. All the effective Christian leaders I know are men and women who are deeply committed to spending time daily with God in his word. Their lives are marked by stability.*
> Jeremiah J. Johnston[8]

Over many years, those offending comments had caused some damage to my self-esteem, but that isn't the reason for sharing my story. It is simply to show you what God reminded me of that week: proactively engaging with his word is far more powerful than self-effort. It is the key that unlocks God's transformation and opens the door to Part II of this book; it is the 'how' to let Jesus transform our thinking and responses, when self-image is dented by pressures, ideals and expectations from secular culture.

The apostle James writes:

> *Do not merely listen to the word, and so deceive yourselves. Do what it says. Anyone who listens to the word but does not do what*

> *it says is like someone who looks at his face in a mirror and, after looking at himself, goes away and immediately forgets what he looks like. But whoever looks intently into the perfect law that gives freedom and continues in it – not forgetting what they have heard but doing it – they will be blessed in what they do.*
> JAMES 1:22–25

Let's take this one step at a time:

Do not merely listen

- Very few people in James' day owned copies of God's word, so they relied on listening to a priest, an apostle or a leader reading it to them. How often do you *listen* to your Bible, either through reading or hearing it?

Do what it says

- 'The wise don't just read their Bible; they let their Bible read them' (anon.)
- Looking back over the past week, how much of what you have heard or read in the Bible has changed how you have spoken, behaved or responded? Be open to God, to inspire or challenge you to 'do it' more.

Looking in the mirror, then forgetting what you look like

- Life offers many mirrors, reflections and messages suggesting who you should be and what you should do. If you look at and listen to the wrong mirrors, it invites abuse to your God-given worth.
- Even if you look at the mirror image and message of Jesus, unless you *do* something with it, you may soon forget what he said, and those other mirrors will jump right in to compete for your attention and response.

Looks intently

- There is a difference between hearing and listening. Hearing is simply perceiving sound. Listening is a conscious choice to concentrate on and pay attention to what you are hearing, so that your brain can process what it means.
- I know the times I open my Bible and just skim over the words, and how different that is to when I read with concerted focus; when I unzip my heart to the whispers of God's Spirit, imparting his image and messages directly to my soul. And that's when I find…

Freedom

- God's truth can permanently set you free from a shackled self-image (John 8:32).
- Focusing on God's word releases you from the power of demeaning messages or unnecessary expectations put on you by our culture; it enables you to experience the abundant spiritual life God intended.
- Jesus is described as the Word that became flesh (John 1:14). As you engage with and respond to scripture, his Spirit will use it to further equip and transform you, enabling you to live well for him and to experience his promise of a fulfilled life, even when dealing with problems and pain.

And continues to do this, not forgetting but doing it

- The Bible often speaks in the ongoing tense: keep on asking; keep on seeking; keep on being filled with the Holy Spirit and pursuing the things of God. So too with God's word: if you keep on focusing on the word it will continually restore your perspective on the value of Christ's image and purpose in your life.
- Even now, many years later, Isaiah 30:15 and 32:17 continue to infuse my life with strength and peace, in scenarios such as the one described above and other situations too. It is when I forget

to respond to these verses that I feel undermined and my old reactions return.

Will be blessed

- '*Will* be blessed'! It's a promise. When you look into the right mirror for the reflected radiance of Christ's character and promise, listening to his messages rather than those of the world, and putting them into practice (see Part II), you *will* experience this promise of blessing. Issues of negative self-image will be disempowered by truth, and replaced with a healthy sense of well-being from who you are in Christ.

But whoever catches a glimpse of the revealed counsel of God – the free life! – even out of the corner of his eye, and sticks with it, is no distracted scatterbrain but a man or woman of action. That person will find delight and affirmation in the action.
JAMES 1:25 (MSG)

I long that this book will help you experience 'delight and affirmation' when you engage proactively with God's word, and 'the free life' that God intended for you, unencumbered by low self-image or the pressure to conform.

But let me highlight one sentence from my opening story: it was because I engaged with Spirit-inspired scripture that 'I experienced a new confidence in who I was in God – a quiet but empowering security that no one else's words or behaviour could undermine'.

I pray that will be your experience too.

Your story

I didn't suddenly know where to look up those references in Isaiah; I was familiar with their existence through years of regular Bible reading, so the Holy Spirit could bring them to mind when I most needed them. Perhaps some of the following ideas may be helpful in reigniting your own reading and response.

I use a Bible guide in conjunction with reading my Bible and try to set a time to read in the morning. When I was on holiday I spent much more time reading, then missed it when I went to work, so decided to get up an extra hour earlier.
Jen

- If you need to make more time to read your Bible, could you set your alarm five minutes earlier? Then next week, set it ten minutes earlier? Then next month…?
- Have you considered using Bible-study notes to help your reading and understanding? There are many styles available both in print and online. Try a new one if you have been put off, but still need help to grapple with God's word in meaningful ways.
- A Bible concordance, handbook and/or encyclopedia (printed or software) can be invaluable to help you understand the Bible's context and message. Birthday or Christmas gift idea, perhaps?

Take another look at Brother Andrew's words, quoted at the beginning of this chapter. I keep a copy of them in whichever page of the Bible I am currently reading. They are a daily reminder to engage, respond and not just read.

- If you think it would help, write them out and pop them in your Bible too.

I make notes when I read the Bible, writing down any revelations I get. I also write down what I understand or don't understand.
Lily

- Perhaps you would like to invest in a new notebook that you can use to journal the verses God speaks to your heart and the situations they are pertinent to.

I use a journalling Bible. I read it before bed and write about a particular verse and how it is personal to me at that time, though often there's not enough space!
Ella

- Would this type of Bible help you engage with God's word more? Another idea for the birthday-gift list, perhaps?

I personally find that seeing is more powerful than just hearing. I have to write out verses and sometimes the prayers people pray for me, so that I can see them. It makes it more meaningful to me.
Yasmin

- Grab a sticky-note pad if this idea would help you too.

My daughter writes out scripture in calligraphy, then spends time developing it into a piece of decorative art. She finds this a helpful way to take time in God's word and absorb its truth.

- Perhaps that might appeal to you too.

Taking it further

Tell me and I forget, teach me and I may remember, involve me and I learn.[9]

God's word is described as:

- refreshing (Psalm 19:7)
- joy-giving (Psalm 19:8)
- precious (Psalm 19:10)
- a lamp and a light (Psalm 119:105)
- being like fire (Jeremiah 23:29)
- being like a hammer (Jeremiah 23:29)
- truth (John 17:17)

- a sword (Ephesians 6:17)
- God-breathed (2 Timothy 3:16)
- useful for teaching, rebuking, correcting, training and equipping (2 Timothy 3:16–17)
- alive and active (Hebrews 4:12)
- sharp and penetrating (Hebrews 4:12)
- a judge of thoughts and attitudes (Hebrews 4:12)

One by one, imagine these objects and attributes at work in everyday life. How does each image inspire you with the power of God's word to destroy lies and bring truth and life to your heart, mind, body, spirit and soul?

Read Psalm 119. Although it is long, it's a wonderful confirmation of the importance of God's word to the writer. Highlight the verses that show this (for example, vv. 2, 9, 11, 97, 105 and 165), and ask God to increase your own passion for his word.

Pause to respond to God

Open my eyes that I may see wonderful things in your law.
PSALM 119:18

Pray this now, and pray it every time you look into God's word.

Role models who inspire for reasons other than their appearance

Here is one from me: Cindy Bauer was one of my lecturers at YWAM (Pahi, New Zealand, 1992). As I listened to her passion for Jesus and her knowledge of the Bible, pouring out of her with deep discernment and authority, I found myself doodling in my notepad: 'I want to be a woman of God like her.'

Footnote: thinking about e-Bibles

I am not against e-Bibles; I use one when I'm on holiday to save me the weight of a book. They can be handy, too, if you want to look up something while you are out and about. But some potential downsides of relying solely on e-Bibles have been suggested.[10]

My only comment is that I don't idolise the paper of my Bible as a religious icon. I've got Marmite stains, scribbled notes and highlighter marker all over it, and if I drop it, I drop it (though I then waste 20 minutes trying to find the right pages among which to replace my many bookmarks and scraps of paper). And yet, when I sit with the weight of God's word on my lap, I feel a great sense of God in this place – like Jacob felt at Bethel (Genesis 28:16–17).

Seeing the whole of the Bible between two covers helps me understand God's story, its chronology and flow, while my scribbled notes and highlighter markings help root his messages deep in my soul, transforming my outlook and responses.

> *Anyone who lives on milk, being still an infant, is not acquainted with the teaching about righteousness. But solid food is for the mature, who by constant use have trained themselves to distinguish good from evil.*
> HEBREWS 5:13–14

Do you want to mature as a woman of God? Then join me in this lifelong process of increasing transformation, as we choose to feed and strengthen our soul with the word that is more than ink on paper, but alive with the breath of God.

ii

The mirror messages

4

Mirror, mirror, on the wall

Body-image issues and self-image

The body is a sacred garment: it is what you enter life in and what you depart life with, and it should be treated with honour, and with joy and with fear as well. But always, though, with blessing.

Martha Graham, dancer and choreographer, 1894–1991

My story

It was past midnight when I slipped off my shoes and climbed the stairs to my bedroom – my refuge from work and the world.

For 19 years it had been my safe space for cuddly toys, playing, diaries and teenage music. It had been the place my mother had nursed me when I was sick and the place to dangle my legs over the window ledge, free to dream a young woman's dreams.

That night, however, was different. Windows and curtains were shut tight against cold, clear skies, and the air was stuffy with beer-breath and sweat. I don't drink beer.

As I closed the bedroom door my fears were confirmed. I could hear his drunken snores. My ex-boyfriend twitched and groaned, but slept on; a long, menacing kitchen knife lay next to him on the carpet – the one Mum used to carve the Sunday joint and sharpened on a whetstone every week. He must have let himself into the house. (We weren't accustomed to locking doors back then – it wasn't necessary; though we did so after that night.)

Tiptoeing across the room I wrapped the knife in a long skirt, then lay it on a shelf beneath a pile of jumpers. I considered calling my parents from their room across the hall, but Shaun (not his real name) was packed tight with gym muscle, and I was afraid for their safety.

And that's when I felt his dark eyes inspecting me. I looked up to find he was wearing his trademark sneer.

'Good time, then? Come over here and sit those legs down next to me.'

I bit my lip, my stomach twisting. How to cajole him to leave without inflaming his temper? He had never liked me going out, but he had hated it even more since we had split up. I think he knew he was losing control, something I had unwittingly let him have. By the time we separated, he controlled how I spent my money, how much time I shared with family, which clothes I wore and what figure I should aspire to. In fact, he controlled how I felt: if he was happy, so was I; if he felt unfit, then I had to diet; if he was angry, I was afraid. I am not saying I was perfect, and I certainly made mistakes, but his dreams had to be my dreams. His way was always right.

He began to sob, begging me to take him back. I was shaking inside but kept on gently coaxing him to leave. A half-hour passed, then another, his endless story cycling round and round, when suddenly he cut off mid-sentence, staggered to his feet and started prowling round the room.

'The knife,' he hissed. 'What have you done with the knife?'

I spluttered some vague reply.

'There's plenty more in the kitchen,' he said. 'You can't hide them all.' And with that, he disappeared.

I was stunned momentarily by his sudden departure, then ran to the door and locked it. I dived into bed fully dressed, hugged myself tight in a foetal position – and waited.

Long minutes later the handle rattled. I could hear hoarse whispers calling my name, then fingernails scratching the door. I pulled the duvet tight round my neck, but then it fell so quiet that I panicked for the safety of my parents.

A pebble rapped against my window, then another. And at last the night fell quiet again. So very quiet.

I woke to the grey light of dawn, terror scourging my soul. I had to check my parents were safe.

'Shaun?' I called softly, tentatively approaching the door.

With a trembling hand I turned the key, then hesitated. But no one forced themselves in on me; there was no sound of the predator stalking outside.

When I dared to crack it open, I saw the door was streaked with blood – the walls down the stairwell too. Crying out, I burst into my parents' room. They were so kind, so concerned, so loving; so shocked that they hadn't heard anything.

Mum held me, rocking me gently against her sleep-snug body. Dad raced downstairs to investigate. I called out to him to be careful, but Mum soothed my fears.

My white car was also streaked red, though Dad kindly washed it off before letting me outside, and we later heard Shaun had suffered only superficial cuts. I think he suffered more from the shame of spending the next night in a police cell.

He had made a grave mistake, but he was still young and evidently full of remorse. We didn't press charges, and he was ordered to never make contact again.

> 'Cursed is the one who trusts in man, who draws strength from mere flesh and whose heart turns away from the Lord.'
> JEREMIAH 17:5

I make no apology for a longer-than-usual story to start this chapter, as that was how my body-image issues began, later spiralling into anorexia nervosa. My weight had been fine until that point, but years of being controlled by someone else's opinions and feelings, then the threat from a blade and the shock of the blood, finally snapped something inside me.

Rather than crumpling, I took control – massive, unhealthy control, as I turned away from God's mirror of truth and trusted in myself. It was the only way I thought I could cope with the haunting memories and the demands still being shouted at me from images in magazines and on TV.

An ongoing problem

Body-image issues vary in effect and intensity, but the problem isn't going away. *The Dove Global Beauty and Confidence Report* (2016), which interviewed women from 13 countries, states:

> *women and girls often have a vexed relationship with their appearance – one that too often prevents them from properly caring for, respecting and existing comfortably in their own*

bodies... Most disturbingly, lack of body confidence has significant public health implications... Furthermore, lack of body confidence is undermining women's and girls' ability to perform to their full potential in important developmental goals and tasks.[11]

Here are some figures:

When women... don't feel good about the way they look:
- *9 in 10 opt out of important life activities, such as engaging with friends and loved ones.*
- *9 in 10 stop themselves from eating or otherwise put their health at risk (e.g. avoid going to the doctor).*
- *5 in 10 have not been assertive in their opinion or stuck to their decision.*[12]

The UK Government also views body-image issues as a public health and equalities issue, contributing to poor mental well-being, eating disorders, obesity, low aspiration, self-harm and alcohol and drug abuse, as well as reinforcing sexual objectification of women and potentially reducing their confidence to achieve in economic, political and social fields.[13]

Body-image issues are not something to be dismissed as a girlish fad or shallow thinking, and the church should certainly not ignore them, as though Christians are immune. In fact, body-image issues can contribute significantly to women failing to experience Christ's promise of living life 'to the full' (John 10:10).

And perhaps you know that applies to you too.

The mirror message of culture

Having a good body image does not mean thinking that you are beautiful (though you are welcome to!); it means appreciating

your body for what it is and does, in healthy balance with all the
attributes and actions that combine to create self-worth.
UK Government Equalities Office, *Body Confidence Campaign*[14]

Body image is how we perceive our body, and how we believe other people perceive it. If we want others to think we are attractive, we check the mirror images and messages of the world, then do whatever we can to match up. But if we fail, or feel unable to make the necessary changes, our perception of being unattractive can make us miserable and think we are inadequate. These beliefs can morph into further problems if we leave them to fester.

The issue is not that each culture has its own ideals of beauty, as that has been true for centuries. The problems come when those ideals are so distorted that we feel worthless or ashamed if we don't measure up, and when we make physical beauty the principal quality in life – what we aspire to and work towards at all costs.

The problem is that we've made a 'god' of our body, hearing and responding to the lie that when we look like 'that' we will feel good in our jeans, bikini, sportswear or ball dress; we will have a better life; we will feel confident, and therefore be more able to fulfil our potential; we will be accepted, wanted and admired by people we want to befriend or impress; we will be loved, cherished and cared for by a wonderful partner. We will at last feel happy.

But perhaps some may say that addressing issues of body image is shallow, vain and self-centred. With the crises of refugees, poverty and sex trafficking, should Christian women even be thinking about body-image matters?

My answer is threefold:

1 If body-image issues are limiting our experience of God's grace and abundant life and are shackling our potential, then, yes, we need to address them.

2 Body image is only a problem when we make our body our god. But this book is about focusing on the one true God, our loving Father, who created us to be content with the body he designed for us.

3 'Love your neighbour as yourself' is the second-greatest commandment (Matthew 22:39), but it is not the same as the warning against being lovers of ourselves (2 Timothy 3:1–5). This is not about body worship; it is about knowing the God-imbued worth of our body. And that is not as easy for some as it sounds.

Your story

I hated being skinny. I still wear baggy clothes to hide it.
Pip

If you struggle with body image, it will take time to heal your wounds as you daily engage with and respond to God's truth, and you will find encouragement to keep doing that throughout this book. But there is an essential first step to make: to immerse not just your head belief, but your whole heart in God's love for the way he made you.

So you have a choice:

1 keep responding much like the people in Isaiah 29:16, which, translated in your heart, might sound something like this:

God, you have no idea how it feels to look like me. What would you know about how I should look or what I should do? Just let me keep doing it my own way. I'll work it out somehow. The mirrors of the world will guide me, even if they deflate me.

I'm sure you wouldn't dream of saying that verbatim, but that's what might be happening deep within your soul, when you allow the world's mirrors to superimpose their own ideals over the design of the one who made you, the one who *loves* what he made.

2 choose to respond as in Isaiah 64:8 (changed to first person singular): 'Yet you, Lord, are my Father. I am the clay, you are the potter; I am the work of your hand.'

This is easy enough to believe in your head, but to help this truth become authentic in your heart take time in the following response, and let God's mirror image and message of truth flood your soul.

Imagine a time before you existed.

See two nail-scarred hands place a lump of clay on a potter's wheel. The wheel spins but the clay remains without form.

Dipping his hands in water, the potter takes firm hold of the clay, spreading strong fingers around it, pushing it up with the heels of his palms, then squeezing it back with his fingers. His thumbs press in, creating an opening.

The potter bends low, his breathing slow and deep through concentration; warm life spreads through the clay as he gently eases it higher, just a little at a time.

His expert fingers keep moving over the clay, designing the unique shape he already has in mind.

The jar grows.

Marvel as he places one hand inside and presses outwards against the other, changing the jar's shape until he sees it is just as he intended.

The intimacy between potter and clay already exists, even in its state of formation. He will always love that jar, even with its potential weaknesses. No matter if chips, cracks or scratches mar its form when it enters the heat of the kiln, its intrinsic value and purpose will never be changed.

The jar swells and shrinks in just the right places for the purpose he longs to use it for.

He smiles, then adds the finishing touches, inscribing his signature into the clay.

This is not conveyor-belt cloning, this is one potter with one lump of clay; there will never be another jar like it.

Let Isaiah's image of potter and clay begin to imbue your distorted body image with the priceless value God places on you. Let his unique design feed your self-worth with purpose. Let his adoring smile blot out the glare of the other mirror images and messages clamouring for your attention.

Taking it further

If someone compliments me I immediately disregard it, and say, or think, that I know they are lying: 'Are you blind? Look at these bacon rolls I'm carrying!'
Amy

We need to stop hating our bodies if we are to find peace with ourselves. Depending on your level of self-hatred, that may take some time. Be kind enough to yourself not to expect too much too soon; love yourself as God does, so that you want to reach out for his healing.

Listen to the Youth Work Resource four-minute reflection called 'the mirrors'.[15] What are your responses to the gentle questioning?

Pause to respond to God

For you created my inmost being; you knit me together in my mother's womb. I praise you because I am fearfully and wonderfully made; your works are wonderful, I know that full well. My frame was not hidden from you when I was made in the secret place, when I was woven together in the depths of the earth. Your eyes saw my unformed body...

PSALM 139:13–16

I know that full well.

- Keep reflecting on the potter while praying this prayer, until its truth is no longer head belief but the overflow from your heart.
- Thank God that he designed you and chose to make you from the quarry of your parents' gene pool, even if you don't know who your parents are or if conception was not their intention.
- Praise him that his work in creating you is and was wonderful, even if it has been scarred by our broken world.
- Worship him in loving response to the endless love he has always had for you since first your unformed body was a longed-for creation in his heart.

Role models who inspire for reasons other than their appearance

My granny is one of my favourite people on this planet, and I aim to grow old with grace like her. She's never had any piercings or dyed her hair, and although I have or will do both of those, I have so much respect that she has never felt the need to, despite the fact both were very fashionable at some point for her generation.

Alice

5

Restoring my true identity

Outward appearance and self-image

Beauty was not a thing that I could acquire or consume, it was something that I just had to be.

Lupita Nyong'o, actor[16]

My story

One of the perks of my job is being able to work in the garden on sunny days, but it is often misunderstood, especially if I answer the door wearing a strappy top, shorts and flip-flops. That's when I hear the kind of response other writer friends have heard, who themselves like to work in pyjamas: 'It's all right for some!' the visitor scoffs. 'I wish I had time to relax.'

In truth, we may have been grappling with theology, struggling to sort ideas or painstakingly searching for just the right words before a pressing deadline. Many of us, however, whatever our work or circumstances, have learned the sad truth that we are often judged by our outward appearance, compelling us to conform to someone else's ideals, to *their* mirror image and message of what is expected, popular or beautiful.

There is a time and place to respect cultural norms, which is why the apostle Paul taught that women in Corinth should cover their heads

(1 Corinthians 11:1–16). It is why I donned a Punjabi outfit while sharing the gospel in India, rather than wearing Western clothing, which some associated with loose living. It is why, when I speak at a conference or meet a publisher, I do not wear the clothes that I would put on to dig horse muck into my vegetable patch – a mark of respect for my God-given work as well as for those I work with! And it is also why I am careful not to wear provocative clothing. We cannot be held responsible for every man's lustful thoughts, but as women of God we are not supposed to intentionally provoke them.

That said, I appreciate the reality of the pressure to fit in, to be liked and admired for how we appear. To be wanted. And until we root our identity in who we are in God, that pressure is hard to ignore.

> *The Lord said to Samuel, 'Do not consider his appearance or his height, for I have rejected him. The Lord does not look at the things people look at. People look at the outward appearance, but the Lord looks at the heart.'*
> 1 SAMUEL 16:7

God looks for inner beauty; a number of familiar scriptures teach about this. But for God's values to infiltrate our values beyond mere head knowledge, we must first root our heart in his love and in who we are in him.

Our need to fit in

> *Our 2013 Girls' Attitudes Survey found that 87% of girls and young women think women are judged more for their appearance than their abilities.*
> Girls' Wellbeing Explored[17]

Personal identity relates to self-image, as it dictates how we see ourselves as a person, as well as in relation to others.

When our identity is rooted in the qualities, character and image of Jesus, we feel secure in who we are – that we are loved and valued and have a significant purpose in life. But we can be tempted to look outside of God for an identity, one which fits in with cultural expectations. And as soon as we fail to match up, our self-esteem and self-worth are undermined with the message that we are not wanted in that particular social group, that we have nothing useful to offer – in short, that we're simply not good enough.

Being recognised as one of the crowd can feed the need for acceptance, as well as empower confidence, but it is a shaky place to root something as important as our identity. Skin wrinkles. Fashion is fickle. Disease and accident take their toll. Make-up is fake – wake up in hospital or the morning after your wedding and, if you had never dared unmask the natural you before, then someone will see your real face for the first time. Depending on how secure you've become in creating that dressed-up image, any unexpected or sudden change may rock your sense of well-being.

The pressure to conform is strong, because we know we get judged by our outward appearance, even as Christians.

> *I wear clothes that give me an identity, which means I wear what everyone else is wearing. It's a big issue, because I'm afraid to stand out. When I go out with my friends, I look at them and think, 'We're all wearing just about the same thing.' I see it too as I pick clothes out from the same shops that they go to.*
> Jess

So, as with all things related to making faith a daily reality, we have to make a choice. Are we going to determine our identity by an ever-changing cultural definition of what is acceptable, subjecting our self-image to the misplaced values of the world? Or are we going to look at God's mirror image and message and let *his* opinion steer our hearts?

Rooting our identity in who we are in God

*I pray that you, being rooted and established in love, may...
grasp how wide and long and high and deep is the love of Christ,
and... know this love that surpasses knowledge – that you may
be filled to the measure of all the fullness of God.*
EPHESIANS 3:17–19

In one of his sermons, Jamie Cox, the leader of my church, used the following illustration. Imagine placing a jug of murky, muddy water beneath a running tap in a sink. At first the clear water mingles with the mud, but the more pure water that pours in, the more it displaces the gunk. In time, it forces it out completely, leaving the jug filled with clear water instead.

I love that image. It reminds us that when we stand beneath the stream of God's love and truth, it begins to displace fears and insecurities – whatever it is that shackles us to a need to conform to cultural ideals. And when we choose to keep immersing ourselves in his love and truth, in time he dispels that cultural pressure completely. God releases us to value, and to live in pure acceptance of, who we are, not how we look.

That is why Part I of this book is so important. Your true identity rests in the character, beauty and purpose of the one in whose likeness you were created and whose image you are predestined to conform to. So take time in the following reflection to consider your identity in God, and let it help release you to be who you were really made to be.

Jesus 'had no beauty or majesty to attract us to him, nothing in his appearance that we should desire him' (Isaiah 53:2), but he was secure in his identity because he knew who he was, where he had come from and where he was going (John 13:3). And Jesus wants to imbue that 'knowingness' into your soul too.

Who am I?

For we are God's handiwork, created in Christ Jesus to do good works, which God prepared in advance for us to do.
EPHESIANS 2:10

- Your life was first envisaged by God to know and enjoy his love, and to use your gifts and experiences for his purpose.
- Absorb this truth; don't just skim read it. You were intended. You are loved, wanted and equipped for purpose.

What are my roots?

'Before I formed you in the womb I knew you, before you were born I set you apart…'
JEREMIAH 1:5

- You were the object of God's choice, to be who you are and fulfil what he designed you to do, before you were conceived. You were foreseen in the Creator-Father heart of God, who chose when you would be born.
- Absorb this truth; don't just skim read it. You are not an accident. You are not unwanted. You were not unplanned by your loving creator, whatever the circumstances of your conception.

Where am I heading?

My Father's house has many rooms; if that were not so, would I have told you that I am going there to prepare a place for you? And if I go and prepare a place for you, I will come back and take you to be with me that you also may be where I am.
JOHN 14:2–3

- We can get so caught up with the here and now, not least the pressure to conform to today's ideals, that we lose sight of our ultimate destination. But setting our eyes on that reality helps loosen our grip on the lure, expectations and false promises of this world's mirrors. I can't do that for you; it is a perspective we must each nurture for ourselves (see also Chapter 13).

- Picture yourself on a road with Jesus. He points to the horizon. Imagine the excitement creasing the corners of his eyes as he tells you about the home he has prepared for you. You may find it hard to conceive of, as you can only picture the world you see now, but he asks you to trust him based on glimpses given to us in his word.[18]

- Absorb this truth; don't just skim read it. Let the truth of your eternal future shed light on your 'now', for that is where your path of life is ultimately heading. How might that change what you prioritise today? How might that devalue some of the things that will soon fade away?

God's mirror image and message

Your beauty should not come from outward adornment, such as elaborate hairstyles and the wearing of gold jewellery or fine clothes. Rather, it should be that of your inner self, the unfading beauty of a gentle and quiet spirit, which is of great worth in God's sight.
1 PETER 3:3–4

The apostle Peter is not teaching that caring for our appearance is wrong, but he is saying that outward beauty is not a godly priority.

Becoming obsessed with our appearance can waste extravagant amounts of time, attention and probably money on something that is artificial, external and offers but a temporary boost to our self-image. But Esther inspires us to root our identity in God. Read her story as soon as you have time – it is only a short book – but for now reflect on the following:

2:7 Esther's outward beauty was simply the key that opened the door to her fulfilling her part in God's will. It was her inward beauty that made more of a long-term impact.

2:9 Hegai was the chief palace pimp. The harem was full of many beautiful women, but some Bible commentators suggest that Esther won his special regard because of her submissive and teachable spirit that is portrayed throughout the story, alongside her patience, courage, obedience, self-sacrifice, integrity, humility, astuteness and perseverance. Outward beauty may attract the lust of men's eyes, but inward beauty stays the course, sheds light into darkness and introduces God's presence into godless environments.

2:12 Esther had to be prepared for her role as Xerxes' queen, and God wants to prepare us for our role too. Are we submitting to the brushstrokes and sculpting of the Holy Spirit, or are our mirrors reflecting the world's beauty ideals, distracting us from fulfilling our potential?

2:17 Esther's crown was a constant reminder of *who* she was and *what* God had asked her to be and do as King Xerxes' wife. We have a royal identity too, as daughters of a heavenly king, whose image we reflect with increasing measure as we root our hearts ever deeper in him. How can we keep reminding ourselves of this truth?

4:8 This is where Esther's story has been heading. Her outward beauty unlocked the door to the harem; her inward beauty gave her access to the king, whose wife she needed to be to intercede for God's people. Imagine if she had been more concerned about her appearance than her potential to save thousands from death! Cultural images and messages will try to distract us from God's values, but be inspired by Esther to keep acting and praying to the beat of God's heart for the vulnerable, poor, oppressed and unsaved.

Your story

Online make-up tutorials are a pain because I don't know what everything is that they're using, like weird sponge things! There's a pressure to do make-up perfectly and always something new to buy. The message seems to be 'You're not in the know, so you're not a real woman.' I know that's not true, but the thought is there, and that in itself is a pressure.
Natalie

- What makes you feel like a 'real woman'? Where do you seek that identity from?
- What messages are trying to distract you from your identity in God?

I feel very self-conscious unless I look like everyone else. It's my way of trying to fit in.
Amy

My younger sister won't come out of her bedroom without make-up, let alone leave the house. I think it's because of what her friends think.
Marie

- What motivates you to choose the clothing you wear? How much or little make-up do you need to feel 'safe' to go out in public?
- What, if any, insecurities do your answers identify? How does this challenge where your dependency lies? How might this encourage you to root your security deeper in the love, value and purpose that Jesus has for you?

Money can be a big thing when you can't afford the decent stuff; the MAC make-up and brushes. I hide my pound-shop brushes.
Jess

Make-up can be an addiction to needing to buy more. You do okay until you see a tutorial and think you 'need' the next thing.
Natalie

- Have you ever asked God how *he* wants you to use the money he entrusts you with?

Taking it further

When we had one non-uniform day a year, it was your opportunity to wear the best stuff you had and reveal who you were. But when I started sixth form, I felt under pressure in the summer to get lots of new and good clothes.
Freya

Clothe yourselves with compassion, kindness, humility, gentleness and patience. Bear with each other and forgive one another if any of you has a grievance against someone. Forgive as the Lord forgave you. And over all these virtues put on love, which binds them all together in perfect unity.
COLOSSIANS 3:12–14

Put on love

- If someone were to remember you in the future or describe you to someone that you had never met, what about you would you want to stand out? Your dress sense, make-up technique or toned figure? Or your generous loving-kindness to people from all walks of life, your gentleness, your integrity, your quiet confidence, your compassion and your care?
- How can you focus on nurturing these qualities of inward beauty, rather than on the outward appearance demanded by the world?

Pause to respond to God

Spend time in the following verses, which teach us to reflect God's beautiful image to the world: Ephesians 5:1-2; Hebrews 12:14; 1 Peter 2:12.

- Worship is more than words; it is proved in action. What might be your worship response to these commands?

Role models who inspire for reasons other than their appearance

It sounds ironic, but I admire people who couldn't care less about their looks, and yet I do the opposite.
Sophie

6

God's purpose despite my health

Health problems and self-image

Our mirror image is the image of God seeded within our souls, regardless of the flesh-tent that clothes us.

Hilary McDowell, dramatist, writer and broadcaster, disabled from birth[19]

My story

I lift up my eyes to the mountains – where does my help come from? My help comes from the Lord… I have calmed and quietened myself, I am like a weaned child with its mother; like a weaned child I am content. [Anne], put your hope in the Lord both now and for evermore… Wait for the Lord; be strong and take heart and wait for the Lord.

PSALM 121:1–2; 131:2–3; 27:14

These verses walked me through a seven-month period of seemingly endless health problems. When my doctor frowned and ordered urgent appointments, sending me to the top of hospital waiting lists, I wondered (among more important things) whether I would ever unpack my Christmas decorations again. It's strange what thoughts come to mind when life might prove shorter than you had expected.

But that was then, and this is now.

Despite their potentially debilitating, painful and embarrassing symptoms, my health issues have had a minor impact on my self-image compared with many phenomenal women. So I am humbled yet grateful to introduce you to some of them. Their wisdom far surpasses my own. In fact, even if we enjoy good health, they still have much to teach us and inspire us with.

Evie's story

At 23, I was sectioned under the Mental Health Act in a secure unit. I was diagnosed with bipolar mania disorder, and this label pushed me into a downward spiral, with feelings of shame and hopelessness dominating my battle.

Mental illness still carries a stigma that in itself affects my self-esteem and self-worth. I have very supportive family and friends, but sometimes find myself wondering if they properly understand the illness and that I never chose to be part of the bipolar brigade!

Bipolar has confused me as to who I actually am; it's like living a dual existence. In times of mania, I'm like Tigger in the Winnie the Pooh stories, bouncing around at high speed in the fast lane. In low times, I'm like Eeyore, each hour so gruelling to get through that it is painful to simply be me – neglecting my appearance when I feel that I'm already written off. At times, I even question my existence, becoming entrenched in suicidal thoughts. So recovery is about taming the highs and mellowing the lows. If only it was that easy.

Two consequences of the illness have especially affected my self-image. First, the medication causes weight gain. This batters my self-worth and body image. Although I smile when I call myself a 'heffalump', it does nothing for my mood, and I wonder what people think about my size. But while medication was once my enemy, it has become my best friend and life-support system.

Second, I am a nurse, so watching the mental-health nurses writing up notes, administering medication, compiling care plans and so on has been hard. It distorts my self-esteem, as it is normally me up there. My purpose, and to a degree my power, gets lost in times like this.

In fact, bipolar has stunted my nursing career, as countless relapses and hospitalisations have caused lengthy periods off work, though prior to this I had never taken a day off sick. One lapse lost me my dream post as a senior chemotherapy nurse, and although I got back into uniform, I felt I had been downgraded when moved to a less-challenging field. It was demoralising. It felt like bipolar was winning the battle.

That said, my insight and understanding have been enriched over the years, and at 28 I've begun to accept who I am. I now realise that fighting and resisting my illness simply contributed to my suffering self-image, so maturity has helped me rationalise rather than react to what bipolar throws at me.

While at first bipolar monopolised me, it progressively became a natural part of me. On reflection, I wouldn't be 'me' without it, ironic as that may sound. It's all about acceptance and adjustment. I am finally satisfied that I am Evie *with* bipolar, not Evie *who is* bipolar.

Katherine's story

Katherine Wolf (her real name), a former model, suffered a stroke in her 20s that almost killed her. It paralysed the right side of her face, leaving her with double vision, with right-ear deafness and unable to walk, talk or swallow.

In an interview with *Christianity Today*, she said:

> I am grateful that the Lord has allowed me to experience suffering at an early age…

When I had the stroke, so much was stripped away in terms of my physical abilities – I couldn't use my hands, couldn't eat, or walk – that my appearance was just one more thing I was dealing with. The beauty stuff wasn't as big of a deal; learning to walk again was a big deal. It put my appearance and beauty in its rightful place…

Tragedy redefines and clarifies everything in your life, and when you are dealing with not mothering your own son, your appearance goes to the back burner…

Outer beauty is fading away as you age, but inner beauty has the potential to continually grow and increase…

We are people made in God's image. We have the glory of God in us and we are his beloved. Nothing else is required from us to be worthy but accepting that he loves us, imperfections and all.[20]

Hilary's story

Hilary McDowell (her real name) was disabled from birth seven times over, but her story of hope and faith in God's enabling power is an inspiring, heart-warming read.

Touched in the womb – and God does not make mistakes. Whatever aspect of a fallen earth contributed to the accident of nature which produced seven handicaps for my life challenge, I know that God's creative touch in the womb turned darkness to light, negative to positive, despair to challenge. I have learnt from hard experience that it is not what happens to us that makes or breaks us, but what we do with it.

Given back to God, any negatives can be transformed into the positive which he had originally intended for the person concerned. In my experience, he fulfils his potential for our lives, not necessarily by removing the difficulties, but by climbing inside them with us and transforming the situation from within.

Her story continues:

[After surgery] it was wonderful to get back home but I had an old and formidable adversary to face in renewed combat: my mirror. You might think that someone who had no reason to be vain in the first place would feel no pain in further-diminished attractiveness. However, it does not quite work that way.

I looked awful. No, that was an understatement. To me, I looked hideous… I had never resembled an angel, but now I was inadvertently doing an excellent impersonation of a Halloween witch…

I thought, what better thing to ask for than the return of your smile?[21]

What can we learn?

There is so much we can learn from these and other women, and I feel sure you will take what is most pertinent to you from their stories. But here are a few key points.

Self-esteem

Evie teaches us the power of accepting, rather than fighting and resisting, an illness, to overcome the negative messages it can play to our self-esteem.

'For in him we live and move and have our being.'… 'We are his offspring.'
ACTS 17:28

Our whole being was created to find meaning and wholeness in relationship with Jesus, with or without health problems. As we choose to look at the truth that he reflects back to us, we learn what it means to truly 'live and move and have our being' in Jesus.

Are we willing to accept who we are in him, while living with the fallout of a broken world?

> It's hard because people don't know that my medical condition can make you big. I've got polycystic ovary syndrome, and one of the symptoms is that it can make you large. I hate going out. My brother wanted to take me out for my 18th, but I hated it. I stand on the bus and think everyone is judging me.
> Amy

Evie, Amy and many of us may worry about what we think people think, regardless of our health, so let's remember two things:

1 Unless they have actually said it, we are only assuming we know what other people are thinking. They might not be!
2 Even if people *are* thinking what we would rather they didn't, their opinion does not have to be our opinion. We can choose whose opinion we adopt, so let's open our ears and heart to God's.

Body image

> But we have this treasure in jars of clay to show that this all-surpassing power is from God and not from us.
> 2 CORINTHIANS 4:7

Evie learned that her medically induced weight gain was better than not being able to function, and Katherine learned to see the good that came out of her stroke. It shifted her perspective on what was important in life, reordering her priorities and putting 'appearance' in the right place. It enforced the message that self-worth is all about a relationship with Jesus.

Let's *choose* to look for our own worth in Jesus, before we are forced to by circumstances outside our control.

Self-worth

'Before I formed you in the womb I knew you, before you were born I set you apart…

'I know the plans I have for you… plans to prosper you and not to harm you, plans to give you hope and a future.'
JEREMIAH 1:5; 29:11

Hilary reminds us to choose how we respond to difficulty and that, despite our illness, the plan God had when he made us does not change, giving us a sense of purpose that nurtures our God-given worth.

Hilary asked God to give her back her smile not to enhance her appearance but so that children who had become frightened of her would still know how much she loved and valued them. In time, her prayer was answered and her 'crooked and crazy'[22] smile returned.

How does Hilary's perspective challenge our motives in prayer, regardless of whether we suffer health problems?

When you ask, you do not receive, because you ask with wrong motives, that you may spend what you get on your pleasures.
JAMES 4:3

The following response from another young woman is also an important reminder:

I suffer with EDS [Ehlers-Danlos syndrome]. I am often tired and in pain, but because I am young, people think I am lazy.
Penny

It is frightening to think how often we may have made someone feel bad because we did not know they had an illness affecting their body or behaviour. Let's determine to avoid that in future.

> '*Do not judge, and you will not be judged. Do not condemn, and you will not be condemned…*'
> LUKE 6:37

Your story

In 2013, the UK Office for National Statistics reported that health was the most important factor related to personal well-being – a fact still reflected in statistics for October 2015 to September 2016.[23]

> *I do have lots of insecurities that make me feel kinda ugly. Things like verrucas, warts, allergies, spots, eczema, veiny legs or bloating. I've wrestled with verrucas for about ten years, with 16 of the things at one point. They really embarrass me and give me this horrible paranoia of spreading my contagious virus! It is mostly a problem if I go to the beach with friends and everyone is barefooted. It definitely gets me down and lowers my self-esteem.*
> Molly

- Even minor health symptoms can undermine self-image. What struck you from the stories that may help you with your own issues?

In her book, Hilary challenges those of us who are healthy to encourage others and to emphasise their ability not their disability.

- Do you know someone who suffers?
- How can you draw alongside them?
- How can you encourage them to be all God has made them to be?

Taking it further

Is anyone among you ill? Let them call the elders of the church to pray over them and anoint them with oil in the name of the Lord.
JAMES 5:14

The Old and New Testaments show how God often healed people, and he still does today. Many people testify to that. Be encouraged to pray for healing.

That said, Jesus did not heal every sick person he came across, but he is still *with us* in our illness.

'So do not fear, for I am with you; do not be dismayed, for I am your God. I will strengthen you and help you; I will uphold you with my righteous right hand.'
ISAIAH 41:10

Paul asked three times for healing, but God knew he would be more empowered for his purpose with a weaker body, because his weakness made him more dependent on God's enabling (2 Corinthians 12:7–10).

- If God hasn't healed you, will you still choose to draw close to him, open your heart to his perspective, seek to know how he wants to empower, equip and use you, and let him strengthen you for that role?

Pause to respond to God

Suffering is not the end of the story. The beauty of the gospel is that we see a better story being written and coming out of our sufferings, which changes the way we live the rest of our lives.
Katherine Wolf[24]

- Reflect on this truth, spoken with grace by a woman who knows what it is to suffer.
- You may not be able to mirror her heart just yet, but talk to God about how you feel, where *you* are at right now.

And remember to immerse yourself in God's word as you respond. If it helps, begin with the scriptures that journeyed with me through poor health (Psalm 27:14; 121; 131).

- Read them. Personalise and pray them. Apply and respond to them. Let them help you draw close to Jesus, and worship. He *is* with you. Right now, and in every moment; in every hospital appointment; in every pain; in every test and result. He is *with* you.
- Draw close to him, trust him; you are still of great worth to him.

Role models who inspire for reasons other than their appearance

Women who battle through difficulties in life, and still stand on their own two feet, stronger.

Penny

7

The endless feed

Social media and self-image

**Don't use social media to impress people;
use it to impact people.**
Dave Willis, pastor[25]

My story

Although I have a Facebook author page to connect with readers, I use my personal Facebook profile to keep up with family and friends who live far away. Twitter, meanwhile, is my office: a vibrant platform to connect and network with others, learn from and be inspired by faith and literary feeds, as well as take in some news and a splash of comical input. When the mood takes me, I also post a glimpse of my country life on Instagram, learning from and sharing with other like-minded souls.

I can't deny it feels nice – good even – to get a like, share, retweet or comment, but unlike many of you I didn't grow up in a social-media world – in a world too often dependent on media images and responses to feed a sense of self-worth.

So this is my prayer for this chapter:

> … *that your love [for God and one another] may abound more and more in knowledge and depth of insight, so that you may be able to discern what is best [in your use of social media] and may be… filled with the fruit of righteousness that comes through Jesus Christ – to the glory and praise of God.*
> PHILIPPIANS 1:9–11

Distinguishing the 'good' from the 'bad'

> *Dove's most recent study is mindful to reflect the positive impact social media has on connecting women, growing their networks, helping them share feelings and experiences, and finding their personal tribes.*[26]

Many of my research respondents agreed that social media offers a place to connect with like minds, learn from each other and, as Charlie infers, be honest in a safe environment:

> *I've read some heart-breaking, agonised accounts, from friends who want to be more open about their struggles with depression. Using social media has helped them rather than held them back from being honest.*
> Charlie

Social media can be helpful for faith issues too, whether people are sharing requests for prayer, suggesting links to helpful Christian blogs or posting insights into scripture:

> *I really appreciate sharing and reading other people's posts of significant Bible verses. It is encouraging and uplifting to 'do' life and faith together, even when we're all in different places.*
> Leya

In fact, the Royal Society for Public Health's *#StatusOfMind* report (2017) suggested four key positive effects of social media:

1 Access to other people's health experiences and expert health information.
2 Emotional support and community building.
3 Self-expression and self-identity.
4 Making, maintaining and building upon relationships.

But the report also states that social media has been described as more addictive than cigarettes and alcohol, and is linked with increased rates of anxiety, depression and poor sleep.[27]

The potential problems of social media

There are so many pitfalls to social media that books have been written about it. I, however, have space for just one short chapter, so let me pinpoint four key issues.

Social media can undermine body image

I know when I look at profile pictures that it's not their usual look, but it can still make me feel worse about how I look.
Clare

Social-media mirror images can make us feel disappointed and even despondent about our appearance, as they tell us we should look like 'that' if we want to be attractive, beautiful, fashionable, sexy, wanted or loved. But most of us cannot look like 'that' – and it challenges our true worth.

Social media can undermine self-esteem

Your profile picture must be the best you can make it. No day-to-day look, and no picture if you've put on weight.
Sophie

I love reading posts from friends and family, seeing what they are up to and who they are with and celebrating new milestones with them, so I'm the first to agree that there is a place for sharing life via social media.

The problem comes when we start comparing ourselves negatively with others or start yearning for what someone else seems to have: *She must be really popular… I would look so lumpy in that outfit… She could be a model… I failed my A levels… If only I had a boyfriend… I'm struggling to conceive… I've miscarried twice… It's all right for some who can afford holidays… I wish our church had flashing lights and loud music; surely God must be far more powerful there than where I go.*

You can't get away from social media's misleading distortions

It is a constant companion. A constant message. That is what has changed. You could put a magazine down, but now you're always looking at your phone through the day.
Chrissie

It is because social media is a constant feed that it has set itself up as a primary mirror image and message to live up to. But it distorts godly priorities, creating stress and negativity which God never intended.

Social media is not intrinsically wrong. The problem is the addiction to keeping up with the feed, and looking to it as our mirror to inform our sense of self-image.

Many of us still contribute to the problem

Social media makes it look like everyone's life is wonderful compared with yours and it makes you feel negative. And yet, I'm no different. I only post the positive stuff about my life too.
Chrissie

We cannot take responsibility for everyone's feelings in response to a post, but that doesn't mean we just carry on posting ad lib regardless of others. So, let's take a look at the issue from God's perspective.

Restoring God's mirror image and message to social media

The rise of social media has made us more self-conscious, with more than half of British women under the age of 40 feeling pressured to present the best possible version of themselves online, which, if liked or commented on, then boosts their confidence.[28]

Or, as Jess translates:

Getting liked for selfies is really important. There's always a target I want to reach, which on Instagram is 100. If I reach it, my friend sends me a message saying, 'Whoa, you did it!'
Jess

This little book is not going to change the fickle nature of social media. But if our heart sincerely pursues God's image and values, he will inspire us to bring light into the dark places, rather than letting that darkness overwhelm our own self-image.

The particular aspect of Christlikeness that dominates here is humility.

- Jesus 'made himself nothing... he humbled himself' (Philippians 2:7–8).

- Jesus' humble image was evident through his life – a man completely transparent with others and quietly secure in who he was. He did not feel the need to tell people about himself, but at every opportunity he showed it to be true in the way he listened to them, related to them, took time to understand them, then spoke guiding truth into their lives (see John 4:4–26).
- He did not have to promote that he was right, or that he had authority to judge; he simply made wise suggestions without shaming or condemning, then let others decide for themselves. In so doing, he released the beauty of God's image in people, through the healing of forgiveness and the grace of his love (see John 8:1–11).
- He did not expect to be served because of who he was, but personally cared and provided for all types of people – even those who might turn against him (see Luke 9:12–17; John 13:1–17).
- He did not go out looking for praise, but when it came his way he received its affirmation, without feeling the need to boast about it to others (see Matthew 16:16–20; John 12:12–15).
- He did not need to prove or justify himself; he was free in who he was to speak the truth and free to be silent. He did not cower before threats, demands, expectations and put-downs, but stood strong in the true image of who he was, even when questioned and intimidated at his farcical trial (see John 18:19–23, 28–40).

In other words, Jesus was so secure in his identity that he felt no need to prove himself or compete with others. So let's think how that might translate to our social-media feed.

Living in a social-media world has taught us to put filters on life – showing people what we want them to see, even if it hides our natural looks, or masks the fact that life is not always a party, is not always steeped in success, is not always happy and healthy, is not always as we had hoped and dreamed it might be.

But humility is transparency – removing the filter to be the real you, the woman who is secure enough in who she is in God to be honest about life's ups and downs and to seek primarily to encourage others.

Such a woman doesn't feel obliged to share every nuance of her personal problems online; she may choose to share, or else prefer to keep those confidences for support 'with flesh on', with people who can genuinely walk her journey with her – even if on occasion that has to be via direct message. But she does let people see her online through the naked lens of who she really is, refusing to filter her image in order to get another shot of the 'like and share' drug. She is confident to post images with or without make-up, dressed up to go out or with blotchy, dry skin. She can share messages celebrating success as well as those that admit to mistakes and disappointment. She is free to encourage others and build them up, while being real about her own low mood or failure. And that is because she's content and secure in who she is, because she looks into the mirror of Jesus.

Your story

Read Philippians 2:1–15 then reflect on how that speaks into your engagement with social media.

> *… being like-minded, having the same love…*
> PHILIPPIANS 2:2

… for God
How might living out your love for God challenge some of the posts you might otherwise be tempted to make?

… for others
The image reflected from a godly, humble heart feels no need to prove itself, compete with others or conform to the expectations of others. How might that also affect what you post?

… for yourself

Loving yourself is intrinsic to the second-greatest commandment (Mark 12:31). When a photo undermines your own body image, when a friend's promotion or exam success shatters your self-esteem, when a wedding announcement or picture of a twelve-week foetal scan rips apart your self-worth, look at the mirror, hear and see Jesus' love for you and receive it to help you love who *you* are.

> *… being one in spirit and of one mind.*
> PHILIPPIANS 2:2

Pray about and reflect on how you can use your time on social media for God, rather than letting social media dictate what you post or control how you feel in response to your feed.

> *Do nothing out of selfish ambition or vain conceit.*
> PHILIPPIANS 2:3

Let go of the need for a certain number of likes as a means to boost your self-esteem.

Humility has nothing to do with dismissing encouragement, and if our desire is to post, like and comment to build others up, then being liked confirms we are doing that. But that is very different from needing lots of 'likes' because we are struggling to find contentment in who God made us to be.

> *Rather, in humility…*
> PHILIPPIANS 2:3

Without comparing, without conforming, without competing, you will no longer be concerned to maintain any image that is anything but the full picture of the real you.

> *… looking… to the interests of the others.*
> PHILIPPIANS 2:4

How can you use social media to encourage others and reveal the true image of God's love and feed into its mega-sphere his truth, wisdom, humour, empathy and grace?

> *… have the same mindset as Christ Jesus…*
> PHILIPPIANS 2:5

As you grow your security in God, your self-image will be healed of social-media insecurities and, in turn, you will shine like a star in a 'warped and crooked generation' (v. 15).

Taking it further

> *We need to start encouraging young women to discover who they are as a whole person and to delight in that. So much of what they experience through social media presents a message of value based on physical appearance. This often leads to low self-esteem, which can lead to mental health issues.*
> Rt Revd Rachel Treweek, Bishop of Gloucester[29]

Dependency is a subtle force; as it grows, it can soon become addiction. God longs for our self-image and well-being to be totally dependent on him. Try the following exercises to check where your dependency lies:

- Leave your phone outside your bedroom at night. If you need an alarm, they can be bought at a pound shop. Notifications (tunes, vibrations or flashing lights) and the temptation to check a feed if you wake in the night hinder you from sinking into the deep sleep that supports mental and physical health.
- Keep your phone switched off (not just muted) when you take your personal time to be quiet with God, and when you are talking with him, listening to him and reading his messages to you. If your only Bible is on your phone – get it in book form. Ask for one as a

gift if you can't afford one, or ask someone at your church if they have spare copies.

- When you go out with friends or family, suggest only *one* of you takes a mobile phone, and only for emergencies. Be present for each other in the time you have together, without the need to take and post photos. Talk with one another, undistracted by feeds. Engage with the unfiltered reality of friendship, food, music and the natural world.
- Try taking a Sabbath – one day per week – when you switch yourself off from the Internet – from websites, blogs, email and all social media. Switch off your notifications on your mobile too.
- Choose not to feel pressured by friends or family if they say, 'Take a look at this post.' Wait until the next day; it will still be there.
- Finding that too hard? That's okay, but recognise your dependency as an issue to be addressed, and try again next week. And the next.

FOMO (fear of missing out) is stressful. But you can know a deep-seated rest for your soul if you keep on pursuing Jesus.

Pause to respond to God

'Are you tired? Worn out? Burned out… Come to me. Get away with me and you'll recover your life. I'll show you how to take a real rest. Walk with me and work with me – watch how I do it. Learn the unforced rhythms of grace. I won't lay anything heavy or ill-fitting on you. Keep company with me and you'll learn to live freely and lightly.'
MATTHEW 11:28–30 (MSG)

Switch off your phone, tablet and laptop. Don't just mute them. Switch them off.

'Come' in your heart, mind, soul and strength to Jesus.

'Get away' from those images, expectations and pressures and the need to be liked.

'Recover your life' as it was created to be, your thoughts stilled and your heart at peace as you 'rest' in God's love and affirmation, letting go of the pressure to *look like* or be *liked*.

Enjoy the 'rhythm' of being released.

Be yourself. Be true to yourself. Be true to how God has made you and the experiences that may be challenging you.

'Keep company' with Jesus for this time, undistracted by electronic feeds and filters. Keep company with Jesus on your Sabbath. Keep company with him, even when that phone gets switched back on.

Role models who inspire for reasons other than their appearance

My mum is an inspiration. She doesn't really care how she looks, and I love that.
Miriam

8

A subjective subject

Success and self-image

Never count success as money gained. That is not the mind of My Kingdom. Your success is the measure of My will and Mind that you have revealed to those around you. Your success is the measure of My will that those around you have seen worked out in your lives.

God Calling, 29 October[30]

My story

I was elated with my grade C in O-level chemistry, as I thought I'd failed the exam. I promptly gave up ever thinking about the subject again, and celebrated by burning my laboratory coat! My friend, however, would have been gutted without her A, but unlike me she was destined to pursue the subject to first-class degree.

Today, a would-be writer might call me successful, as my work has been published as Bible notes, articles and books, but authors with multimillion sales would scorn the 'success' of my few thousand copies sold. For someone else, success may be earning enough to pay the rent and put food on the table, while for another it's the reward of a bonus for work well done, despite already earning a substantial salary.

As you can see, our understanding of the word success is highly subjective, another distorted mirror we can be tempted to look into to gauge how well we measure up. And if we fail to achieve our goals or meet the expectations of those we want to impress, it can quickly cripple our self-image.

There are two questions we need to ask the mirror of truth in God's word:

1 What is God's definition of success?
2 Has God promised us success in a specific area?

When we know those answers, we can be 'confident of this, that he who began a good work in [us] will carry it on to completion until the day of Christ Jesus' (Philippians 1:6).

First, let's remind ourselves why focusing on success as our culture defines it can be so damaging to self-image.

The pitfalls of our cultural definition of success

Success isn't up for comparisons

My self-esteem took a battering when I felt that doing a college course wasn't as good as going to university; not because others said it, but it was how I felt. And it pulled me down.
Jen

When we start comparing what we are doing or achieving with someone else's life, it either fosters pride if we feel we're doing better or else undermines our self-image if we feel that we're not as good.

While another person's success can help motivate us to pursue our goals, God never intended that their achievement should grade our own level of worth.

Success can be distorted by perfectionism

Nearly 8 in 10 (78%) of both women and girls feel under pressure to never make mistakes or show weakness.[31]

The perfectionist forgets that failure can be the best teacher. It can guide us on to a more suitable path or teach us important lessons to apply at our next attempt. Failure is only an enemy if we do not learn something from it or allow it to put us off trying again.

What's more, God never intended mistakes and failure to cripple our self-image. After all, he chooses to use the imperfect you and me in his work in this world. We are not protected from failing by having a God-centred self-image, but it will give us confidence to ask what we can learn and what steps to take next.

Success is often temporary, fickle or vacillating

Our greatest fear should not be of failure, but of succeeding at something that doesn't really matter.
D.L. Moody

It is the praise, admiration or financial reward (or some other commendation) that accompanies success that helps feed our need to feel capable, valued, respected and wanted. But the opposite is also true.

One of my books received a couple of reviews that were so complimentary they were worth hanging on the wall! But my bloated self-image ruptured unceremoniously when I saw a third review that was nothing short of rude and humiliating. Cringing behind my sense of failure and incompetency, I never wanted to go outside again, let alone write.

But God never intended for our sense of well-being to depend on subjective human opinion.

Success is not always possible

I feel I have failed because I haven't achieved what I wanted to achieve, even though I've been held back by illness.
Evie

Feeling held back from fulfilling our dreams by illness, redundancy or simply coming to the realisation that we're not capable of achieving the success we had hoped for can be devastating to our self-image; despite giving something the best of our time and effort we are still not good enough. Our confidence gets knocked, and insecurity sneaks in, followed fast by its best friend, worthlessness.

But God did not design self-image to be rooted in goals he never asked us to achieve or in fulfilling dreams that can no longer be part of our changing circumstances.

God *does* want us to be successful in our place in this world, but nurturing a steady and healthy self-image relies on us pursuing success as he defines it.

God's mirror image and message

'Seek first the kingdom of God…'
MATTHEW 6:33 (ESV)

We are 'Christ's ambassadors' (2 Corinthians 5:20); we are vessels of the Holy Spirit to reveal the reality of God's presence and convey his truth to the world. This is our priority – to seek to live in such a way that makes him known, in whatever situations we find ourselves and whoever we are with.

Success, as God defines it, is therefore like two sides of the same coin. On one side, we have the ongoing work of the Holy Spirit, transforming us increasingly into Christ's likeness, that we may bear spiritual fruit which reveals God's 'love, joy, peace, forbearance, kindness, goodness, faithfulness, gentleness and self-control' (Galatians 5:22–23). On the other side of the coin, we have God's empowering to enable and anoint us to succeed in his work. Paul writes, 'it is *God* who works *in* you to will and to act in order to fulfil his good purpose' (Philippians 2:13, my italics). And Hebrews 13:20–21 asks God to equip us with everything we need to do his will. Godly success is not about our capability, but our availability and our readiness through a surrendered heart, rooted in the word and prayer.

> *'No branch can bear fruit by itself; it must remain in the vine. Neither can you bear fruit unless you remain in me... apart from me you can do nothing.'*
> JOHN 15:4–5

This kind of success cannot be graded with a mark out of ten, because we will never know the full extent of our influence. If we did, it might feed our pride and bloat an unhealthy self-image, just like other benchmarks of success. Exam results, financial reward, promotion or increased book sales may well be part of the outworking of God's purpose through us, but let's not look to our natural talents as our sole source of significance; rather let's look to the one who gave them to us in the first place.

Has God promised me success in something specific?

To answer the second question proposed in 'My story', I've turned to Joshua for help (see Joshua 1:1–9).

Joshua was promised success in battle to take the promised land from the enemy (v. 8). But the promise came with conditions. Perhaps you can pinpoint a specific promise to you, from a time, place or word from God, but you're still waiting for its fulfilment. If so, reflect on the guidelines given to Joshua, and how they might speak into your situation.

> *Be careful to obey all the law... that you may be successful wherever you go... meditate on it day and night, so that you may be careful to do everything written in it. Then you will be prosperous and successful.*
> JOSHUA 1:7–8

The fulfilment of God's promise required Joshua to read God's word, meditate on it and aim to live his life in obedience to its commands. He still had to practice with sword, sling, bow and axe, sharpen the blades, devise battle strategies, and train an army of peasants for war, but primarily he had to know and live out God's word.

You too may need to study for exams, learn and practise skills, or give effort and attention to some other pursuit in becoming who God has called you to be. But when you immerse yourself in God's word, memorising and living by it, this will keep God's kingdom purpose in focus, inspiring you to give your best effort, time, resources and talents to achieve his goals.

> *Be strong and courageous... Be strong and very courageous... Do not be afraid; do not be discouraged...*
> JOSHUA 1:6, 7, 9

God also commanded Joshua to set aside fears, doubts or apathy, in order to release the promised success of conquering the land.

Whether you feel scared, reluctant or tempted to hold back, bear in mind that God needs you to do your part. But as you put your confidence in him, rather than yourself, and as you commit to following his guidance, his promise to equip you will be fulfilled. The only question remaining is will you prove faithful to what he has entrusted you to do (1 Corinthians 4:2)?

> *I will be with you; I will never leave you nor forsake you… the*
> *Lord your God will be with you wherever you go.*
> JOSHUA 1:5, 9

The sustaining component of the promise. Be encouraged. God has promised to remain with you as he remained with Joshua (Hebrews 13:5), to transform, anoint and empower and so enable *his* work in and through you.

Let this inspire you to fulfil whatever he has asked you to do and in turn, realise his promised success.

The reason for the promise

God promised Joshua a land of abundance – 'flowing with milk and honey' (Exodus 3:17); a place of luscious fruit, whose grapevines were so large they had to be carried by two men (Numbers 13:23); a place from which his people would be a blessing to everyone else (Genesis 22:18).

God is promising you a 'promised land' too – a place where your natural physical life dovetails perfectly with your spiritual life. It is the sphere of life that nurtures ample fruit, empowered by the Holy Spirit; the life of God which flows with the riches of spiritual gifts and equipping (1 Corinthians 12:4–6).

But you still live in an imperfect world with its adverse effects and consequences. So when you have done what God has asked you to, to the best of your potential, you can trust him with the outcome. There is no undermining of your self-image if what you had envisioned does not work out. You can be at peace when that grade is not as high as you had hoped, with that failed job application, or when the person you have been witnessing to still chooses not to believe.

Digging and planting in sun-baked soil that is full of weeds is hard work, and it takes time for the harvest to grow – even in the promised land. So don't be too hard on yourself when godly success doesn't happen overnight. God is growing and preparing you, even when you can't see any results. But the harvest will come. His impact and influence through your life will bear fruit for his kingdom, even if you never see it for yourself.

And that is ultimate success – that which will nurture a healthy sense of self-esteem and self-worth.

Your story

Am I now trying to win the approval of human beings, or of God? Or am I trying to please people? If I were still trying to please people, I would not be a servant of Christ.
GALATIANS 1:10

What are you aiming for? What would success look like for you?

Consider your primary motives:

- Are you trying to win the approval of others, which in turn will feed your self-esteem?
- Are you trying to prove yourself worthy?
- Are you driven to earn a level of income that exceeds God's means of providing for you?
- Does your heart beat in time to God's for the souls of the unsaved?

How does God want to work through your circumstances, interests, experiences, skills and gifts?

- Pray before you work. Connect your heart and mind with the Holy Spirit in you. Lean on Jesus and open yourself to be empowered for the task. See yourself not so much as working 'for' God, but presenting yourself as open and available for God to work through you.

- 'Do not neglect your gift' (1 Timothy 4:14). What has God anointed you to do in the power of his Spirit? Are you stepping out in faith to use your spiritual gift?

Is there anything that has undermined your self-esteem because when you tried to do it, you didn't do very well?

- Is this something God wants you to practise and pursue?
- Is this something in which God wants you to rely more heavily on him for empowering?
- Or is this something you need to let go of? If so, be true to yourself; be true to who God created you to be and accept that you cannot do everything. Talk to him about your disappointment, then open your hands and ask him to help you let go of that dream, and release you from any labels such as 'inadequate' or 'failure'.

How can your life 'be for the praise of [God's] glory' today? How can you live 'to the praise of his glory' this week (Ephesians 1:12, 14)?

- How can your words and actions impact and influence others for God, no matter your mood or circumstances?

Taking it further

'My grace is sufficient for you, for my power is made perfect in weakness.'
2 CORINTHIANS 12:9

God does not always ask us to do something that we feel able to do, but are you willing to step out of your comfort zone in faith? Are you prepared to trust God to empower you for the task, as you depend on him each step of the way?

Paul learned this when he asked God to remove a weakness, one that he felt was hampering his work (possibly some kind of ailment: 2 Corinthians 12:7–9). When the problem remained, Paul had two choices: stop doing the work or lean more heavily on God. He chose the latter, and realised that to do that was a far greater answer to his prayer to be empowered for God's work than if the issue had been resolved.

- What about you?

Pause to respond to God

Ours is not to seek praise (for success), ours is to direct that praise to God, for all he has provided and enabled us to do.

Sing out your praise. Give all that you are in abandoned worship. If it helps, join in with the song 'Endless Praise' by Planetshakers, on YouTube (www.youtube.com/watch?v=eHPht8UrPWM).

Start praying this prayer on a regular basis:

May the God of peace equip me with everything good for doing his will, and may he work in me what is pleasing to him, through Jesus Christ, to whom be glory for ever and ever. Amen
Adapted from Hebrews 13:20–21

Role models who inspire for reasons other than their appearance

My mum. She has a tough job, but her faith motivates her to keep doing it because she believes she is there for a reason.
Marie

9

Restoring my first love

Relationships and self-image

We can't change other people but we can change the way we respond to them and the extent to which we allow their words or actions to impact.

Maria Rodrigues, producer and presenter on Premier Christian Radio[32]

My story

We had been together for three-and-a-half years. Even I could hear the wedding bells close friends anticipated, and I would have willingly married him but for one thing. A niggle. An unsettled heart.

I had come to faith and been baptised, but had lapsed in my commitment by the time he appeared in my life. Doting, loving, kind – he couldn't have been more different to my previous partner.

When I later recommitted my heart to Jesus, I prayed and waited for my man to accept him too. He listened to my beliefs and came to a few Christian events. But Jesus wasn't for him. So when marriage began to filter ever so subtly through my thinking, I had to address that niggle.

In my heart, I knew I couldn't marry a man who did not share my faith, even though I knew of some women who appeared to be happily married to non-Christians. Consequently, I had to make a choice: would I fully commit to the God who called me to love him with *all* my heart, or to someone who couldn't decide if God even existed?

It was the most painful decision I have ever made. If I let him go, I would be alone again. I would say goodbye to a potentially good marriage. I would turn my back on the prosperous living his rising career promised. I would choose to reject someone I loved and cared for, and hurt the man who loved me too.

An empty future loomed large; clouds of regret darkened the horizon.

I cried myself to sleep for months, and felt guilty for the pain I'd caused by being obedient to God. But at some point I found myself reading Psalm 63, and it was the first time I had ever made scripture my own: replacing its words with my own name and situation, grappling with it in tearful prayer, kneeling by my bed as a desperate sign that I really meant business, lifting weak hands as I cried out for God to fulfil his word to my heart.

> *You, God, are my God… I thirst for you, my whole being longs for you, in a dry and parched land… On my bed I remember you… I cling to you…*
> PSALM 63:1, 6, 8

Night after night, soaking the duvet cover in tears, I prayed this psalm in my own words. I made its truth mine. I clung on in faith.

When you plant a seed, the seedling can take weeks to appear, and months or years to mature. But I was planting a seed of trust which grew as a result of God's comfort and strength, then enabled me to move on with the life that he had chosen for me; one without that relationship holding me back.

*I will praise you... I will be satisfied... your right hand upholds
me.*
PSALM 63:4, 5, 8

Rooting your self-image in the right place

God was doing two things when he led me to break up that
relationship.

First, he was releasing me from a path of life that was not his
purpose, which in hindsight is so obvious when I look at the work
God had planned for me and at the unfailing support and passionate
love of the man sold out for God who I was later to marry – my
amazing partner, confidante and very best friend.

Second, he was challenging me to look at who was feeding my need
to feel valued and wanted, whose opinions were most important
to me, whose praise I most longed to hear, whose identity I had
adopted and whose expectations I wanted to meet. In short, he was
asking whose presence made me feel most secure, and who it was I
relied on to meet my deepest needs.

That is why I shared my story.

God is not asking you to break up a relationship just because he asked
me to. But he may be asking you to take an honest look at which
relationship(s) you are depending on to feed your self-esteem and
self-worth, rather than finding security in your relationship with him.

It is very easy to believe in our heads that we depend on God, but that
is tested when a significant other – a close friend, parent or partner,
for example – makes negative comments about us, says something
inaccurate, breaks a confidence, puts unnecessary expectations on
us, shows disapproval or disappointment, or can no longer be there
for us.

Relationships are a God-given gift to encourage, support, provide, teach, guide, love and affirm us, among many other things. But no one is perfect. Although God definitely ministers to us through others, he wants us to find unrivalled love, worth, meaning and security primarily in him.

Women who have rooted their security deep into their relationship with God:

- Live with a quiet but determined confidence to be all he made them to be.
- Can give themselves fully to others, because they make no demands on those people to feed their own emotional needs to feel loved, valued or significant.
- Nurture their self-image from God's love and purpose, not by whether others admire, respect, want or praise them; they are encouraged by praise, but not dependent on it to feel good.
- Recognise God's patience with and forgiveness of their own faults, which in turn deepens their gracious forbearance with others who struggle with life's scars and wounds.
- Have firmly established their identity in knowing and relating to God as a Father who loves them unconditionally, values who he made them to be and equips them to fulfil his purpose.

And they get to that place by rooting themselves in truth. Never underestimate the power of God's word to transform your inward being. It is dynamite!

My soul will be satisfied as with the richest of foods.
PSALM 63:5

Your relationship with God is the mirror image and message he wants you to root yourself in – his source of wholeness for your self-esteem and self-worth. I appreciate that may not happen overnight, but I hope 'Your story' will help you engage with and apply this truth for yourself.

Your story

> *When people use negative words about me, I feel silly, a failure,*
> *inadequate. It might be comments from my friends, but also lack*
> *of encouragement from my family.*
> Penny

Identify exactly what was said that undermined your self-image, and
ask God for the truth in his word on the matter. Receive it, believe
it, respond to it and forgive those who have hurt you. If the words
that hurt you were said intentionally, it may be that the person was
feeling insecure, and by putting you down they were trying to build
themselves up. Forgive them, and pray for them to find their security
in God.

> *My friends' opinions of me affect whether I feel good or bad*
> *about myself.*
> Alice

If you speak or behave hypocritically, unkindly or in any way out of
line with God's character and word, it might help to listen to a good
friend's opinion. *Good* friends can be trusted.

But if your friends' negative opinions are just personal views on your
outfit, the subjects you want to study or the job you aspire to, refuse
to let those opinions override who God made you to be. Only you
have the choice to let an opinion undermine you; no one else can
decide that on your behalf.

> *Absence of a boyfriend and doubt it will ever happen makes me*
> *feel unlovable and inadequate.*
> Evie

Trusting God with our deepest desires isn't easy. So, if you feel stuck
in a place of longing but with no reassurance of it being fulfilled, look
again at Psalm 37.

Trust in the Lord…
PSALM 37:3

This is your first choice, to trust in God's love for you, and the good he wants to work in and through your life; the riches of life in him that he longs to give you. Trust that he *will* direct your paths and relationships in his own time.

Take delight in the Lord, and he will give you the desires of your heart.
PSALM 37:4

Note the order. It does not say God will give you your desires *so that* you can delight in him! But as you choose to nurture your relationship with him, his Spirit will be at work in you, transforming your heart so that his desires become your desires. And when that happens, you can be sure he wants to fulfil them.

Commit your way to the Lord… Be still before the Lord and wait patiently for him…
PSALM 37: 5, 7

Commit your life again to God's purpose, and a future he has yet to reveal to you. Be still. Be patient for God to work his heart into yours. And remember, God has a purpose for you right now. Live in this moment, rooting your self-worth in his love, comforted by engaging with his presence, inspired to pursue all he has put on your heart.

No sex before marriage seemed to be the big issue for Christian teaching at church, but once I'd left sixth form, I read stuff that helped me understand why. I now realise that it's not just a rule but it's for my best.
Jen

Sexual promiscuity often reflects a low self-worth, as it can fill our need to feel loved, wanted, accepted or 'normal' by cultural standards. But it is not the way to feed our self-image, and it can be damaging. For God teaches that sex is a gift for marriage (see, for example, 1 Corinthians 7:2, 8–9).

The pain sears far deeper into your soul when a relationship breaks up with someone you have given your most intimate gift to than with someone you haven't. Furthermore, extramarital sex carries an increased risk from sexually transmitted diseases, and it can cause marital problems, be that from jealousy over previous sexual partners or through giving rise to a higher potential for future adultery.

Remember, if someone loves you with *God's* love, they will not pressurise you to prove your love with sex, they will not cajole you to think it is acceptable now you're engaged (after all, you are still not married!) and they certainly won't threaten to dump you.

God's instructions for life are for your good. Hold on to that.

> *Ever since I was little people have left me. My dad left when Mum was 20 weeks pregnant with me. I was adopted by the man she later married, but he eventually left too, then wrote me a letter saying he couldn't visit any more. And my grandad died – the most amazing guy, best friend, dad and grandad. I fell out with Mum and was taken into care; it was horrible and luckily only for six months, but that was hard enough.*
> Amy

Rejection, unfaithfulness and abandonment often lead to the development of trust issues in the recipient, while verbal and physical abuse undermine self-image with shame, humiliation and fear.

Rooting yourself in God's perfect love is powerful enough to drive out your fears and shame, but it's not an easy step to take when you've suffered as much as Amy. So be kind to yourself. And give yourself time. God has promised he will *never* leave or abandon you; he is there for you every minute of every day and night (Hebrews 13:5–6).

Sometimes it helps to meet an experienced counsellor – someone to help open your heart and bare your soul to God's truth. Ask a trusted, godly friend to help you find the support you may need.

Taking it further

The Lord is close to the broken-hearted and saves those who are crushed in spirit.
PSALM 34:18

Consider how God could use *you* to convey his message of wholeness and love to the hurting.

If one of my close friends treats me badly, it can leave me questioning myself, as I can sometimes determine self-value by how I'm treated.
Lily

Others will determine self-value by how *you* treat them too. Read these passages slowly and prayerfully, inviting God to speak to you about your response: Galatians 5:22–23; Colossians 3:12–14; 1 Corinthians 13:4–7.

● How can you build up others with God's love and value for them?

The biggest 'giant I have to slay' is loneliness.
Penny

In 2010, the Mental Health Foundation found that 18-to-34-year-olds were more likely to feel depressed because of loneliness than the over-55s. Chronic loneliness has been linked to depression, anxiety, paranoia and bulimia nervosa, as well as risky behaviour such as increased alcohol consumption, unhealthy eating habits, multiple sexual partners and drug abuse. It is also a known factor in suicide. Low self-esteem is one of the elements that can exacerbate the problem.[33]

'God sets the lonely in families' (Psalm 68:6), so let's pray to know who those lonely people may be in our own church, social, work and neighbourhood environments. Who could we invite for a coffee, a meal, a summer barbecue or a Christmas party? Who could we include in social gatherings and events? Who could we reach out to with friendship and hospitality – and not just once – to give them the 'family' God intended?

> My self-worth gets knocked when people are afraid or uncomfortable and embarrassed to talk to me, just because they aren't sure which twin I am, and assume I'd be offended.
> Molly

There are many reasons we might struggle to go and talk to someone. We see them sitting alone, nursing a mug of tea at church, or munching a sandwich while gazing out of the window at school or work. But we don't know them – they look different to us, they seem more intelligent, they look ragged, we're not sure if they speak English; or else they have serious health problems or have recently been bereaved, and we just don't know what to say.

There are lots of reasons why we leave them alone, afraid for ourselves as much as for them, leaving them to go home with their self-image knocked, just because no one came up to say, 'Hi'.

Let's be sure to change that in future. Let's ask God to fill us with his love and understanding, and trust he will encourage others as we reach out to them.

Pause to respond to God

Commit these prayers to heart. Make them yours. Make them your first focus of the day, but pray them through the day too:

Whom have I in heaven but you? And earth has nothing I desire besides you.
PSALM 73:25

Satisfy [me] in the morning with your unfailing love…
PSALM 90:14

Role models who inspire for reasons other than their appearance

My mum, because she is such a strong woman and the kindest and most selfless person I know.
Amelia

10

A twist in the tale

Faith and self-image

Man's chief end is to glorify God and enjoy him forever.
Westminster Shorter Catechism

My story

I wasn't brought up in a Christian home, so my knowledge of faith was scant. I heard occasional stories about God creating Adam and Eve, and of Jesus being born in a manger then dying on a cross, and I imagined God as an ancient wizard with a long grey beard, leaning on a staff as he surveyed his world from a fluffy white cloud. The input of hymns and recitations of the Lord's Prayer in school assemblies and carol services fed a vague belief in the existence of God, so I assumed I was a Christian.

Then, in my mid-teens, a friend argued that just believing in God was not enough to go to heaven. (Yes, he was that blunt.) Determined to prove him wrong, I visited a church with my mum, but by the end of the service I knew my friend had been right – except that something had changed. Now I really was a Christian, as I had given my life to Jesus during that service!

This was great news for my mum, who was on her own journey of faith, and unbelievable news for my friend.

But it was not such good news for my atheist dad.

My dad was knowledgeable about science, with a keen interest in evolution, so he decimated my new-found faith in the creator God. I had no understanding of who Jesus was, how the Bible had come about or why there seemed to be contradictions in it. Nor could I explain why this all-powerful, loving God would sit back and allow so much human suffering. When friends joined in with their derogatory opinions, I soon felt like a peg hammered into hard-baked ground, unable to resist clever reasoning as I sank beneath the blows of being called naive, silly, ignorant, gullible, shallow, happy-clappy or brainwashed. Shame engulfed me. And although the seeds of doubt never stopped me believing, they did wreck my confidence in talking about my faith.

That was then, but this is now: and 'this is no cause for shame, because I know whom I have believed…' (2 Timothy 1:12).

I now see that 'battering' as a gift. It made me dig deep for understanding and, in turn, it reinforced rather than weakened my beliefs. Although I still long and pray for Dad's eyes to be opened to truth, I am grateful that his opinions drove me to research and think through my faith, rather than accept what I was taught at face value; to prove to myself as much as to him that I was not being brainwashed.

There are certain things about faith that are beyond explanation – which is why it is called faith! Scripture also encourages us to trust God for words of witness when we need them in tense situations (Matthew 10:19–20). But so many of the questions and arguments hurled at us do have answers, so if someone puts you down, see it for the gift that it is – to encourage you to know why you believe what you do. It will help you to relax, inspire you to share confidently in the future, and bring wholeness to your self-image if it was damaged by their unbelief.

When a negative response to faith undermines our self-image

My parents are Christians but my elder brothers stopped going to church when they were in their early teens. I was much younger than them, and they teased me for going. Consequently, I stopped talking to my friends about church as I didn't want them to tease me too.

Chrissie

Teasing is a form of ridicule, so it can undermine your self-image if it makes you feel stupid, belittled or weird. But be true to your beliefs, or else you give our spiritual enemy exactly what he wants: fear that stops you being honest about God or authentic in your behaviour.

Confidence to be real about faith will grow as you engage with today's cynical culture, addressing its questions and misunderstandings rather than hiding or running away. Look out for the many books, blogs and conferences that offer helpful teaching on this.

The apostle Peter said, 'Always be prepared to give an answer to everyone who asks you to give the reason for the hope that you have. But do this with gentleness and respect' (1 Peter 3:15). Your friends may respect your ability to discuss their opinions, even if they choose not to believe. But if the discussion gets heated, don't yell back; agree to disagree until the next opportunity. God doesn't want you to quarrel (2 Timothy 2:24–26), but you can still be praying for your friends, 'keeping a clear conscience, so that those who speak maliciously against your good behaviour in Christ may be ashamed of their slander' (1 Peter 3:16).

I struggle with how to deal with the perception my friends have of church. They judge Christianity based on church stereotypes: of hymns, organs, ancient vicars, and a congregation over 60, but my church is nothing like that.

Alice

I know some fabulous, older, Spirit-filled believers who are active in reaching out to and serving their communities, have the wisdom of years of experience to pass on and are vital pillars of prayer. Sometimes, however, their traditions and preferred style of worship can be too difficult for younger people to relate to. That is why your unsaved friends may get the wrong impression, but don't let that undermine or mask the reality of how *you* join with others to worship God.

Tweet, Facebook, Instagram and Snapchat messages and images of your church events and activities. Play the music that inspires you when your friends come to your home. Invite the sceptics to a social with your Christian friends or to experience the reality of what *you* know as church. After all, look what happened when my friend challenged my misconceptions!

Be the answer to – not the victim of – your friends' misunderstandings, and show them that, while God is unchanging, he is more than able to relate to changing generations.

> *It seems that when someone knows you're a Christian they always bring up the 'no sex before marriage' card – it's their first thought about what Christianity means. They use it against you and it affects your self-esteem as you're not 'normal'.*
> Sammie

Read the section on sex outside of marriage in Chapter 9. Give your friends reasons why you believe it is better for you to wait. And remember: while this may not be normal in the mirrors of our culture, it *is* normal when looking into the mirror image and message of God's truth. As you continue to build your self-image from your identity in God, his normal will become your normal.

> *I don't act like a Christian at college because I want to fit in. I don't want to be ridiculed although I will stand up for someone if they are being put down.*
> Amy

Humans have an innate need to belong, so feeling as if you don't fit in may undermine your self-image.

It is important to be part of non-believing friendship groups, because that is exactly where Jesus wants you to be (Mark 2:17). But as you root your identity and security in your Father's love, and the life he has called you to live, be encouraged to be the *you* he has called you to be, rather than merge with the crowd.

If someone thinks the worst of you for choosing not to behave in a certain way, then remind yourself that it is God you want to please. Let go of their opinion, rather than letting it undermine you (Galatians 1:10), for you are here 'to be salt-seasoning that brings out the God-flavours of this earth... to be light, bringing out the God-colours in the world' (Matthew 5:13–14, MSG).

And remember, if you ever feel things are getting out of control, then walk away. Go home. Protect yourself, as well as the name of Christ, who you identify with.

Lot in Sodom, the prophet Jeremiah, Jesus, the apostle Paul and the early church had to accept their beliefs and lifestyle would not fit well with their culture, might not always be acceptable and could cause them immense hardship – even cost them their lives. And thousands of persecuted Christians today still do. Again, we have to make a choice if what we believe is more important to us than how other people respond, and to root our security and self-image in the truth of who God says we are and who he wants us to be.

Reflecting God's truth

Read 2 Timothy 1:1–12 then consider the following:

> *... fan into flame the gift of God, which is in you...*
> 2 TIMOTHY 1:6

Is your faith just a flicker? Have you allowed God's Spirit in you to be smothered by belittling comments, rejection or fear? Do you want to experience his greater empowering? Then choose to set your mind and heart on the truth of who God is, rather than on someone's unbelief. Nurture your connection with God through prayer, your love for him through devotion and your commitment to him through a proactive response to his word.

> … the Spirit God gave us does not make us timid, but gives us power, love and self-discipline [sound judgment].
> 2 TIMOTHY 1:7

Memorise this verse. It will equip you with confidence when you might otherwise feel reticent or afraid with unsaved friends. God's incredible power is within you through his Spirit.

Look at your friends through God's eyes of love. See beyond the facade of unbelief or ungodly behaviour to the person God loves and longs for them to be. Pray for clear guidance, to know how you can play your part in helping them come to know him.

> … do not be ashamed of the testimony about our Lord…
> 2 TIMOTHY 1:8

The apostle Paul knew Timothy might feel inferior in the face of clever argument, or be unwilling to share about Jesus through fear of being humiliated. But skip on a few verses to where he says:

> … this is no cause for shame, because I know whom I have believed…
> 2 TIMOTHY 1:12

I feared the humiliation of being belittled when sharing about my beliefs until I grew deeper in my relationship with God through prayer, experience of his power as I obeyed his word, and knowledge of the evidence there is for Christ's life and resurrection, the authenticity of the Bible being the word of God, and some of the answers to questions that repeatedly crop up, such as why a God of love allows suffering.

Know who you believe in. Prove who you believe in by a faithful pro-active response. Show confidence in your belief by applying yourself to learning more about your faith. You do not need to be a gifted apologist, but you can benefit from the wisdom of those who are.

> *... join with me in suffering for the gospel, by the power of God.*
> 2 TIMOTHY 1:8

You will still encounter ridicule, and possibly rejection or hardship, for your faith or godly behaviour; it is a fact of life in a world under the dominion of a spiritual enemy, who influences so many against Jesus (Matthew 10:22). But turn your eyes to look into the mirror of God's love, the presence of the image of Jesus within and beside you, and strengthen the roots of your well-being in God's messages to your soul.

> *... called... to a holy life...*
> 2 TIMOTHY 1:9

It is exciting to pursue God-given work and responsibilities, as it imbues life with purpose, which in turn nurtures godly self-esteem. But you are also called to be the image of Jesus to your generation – to devote yourself to a lifestyle set apart and distinguishable from cultural norms.

> *Make every effort to live in peace with everyone and to be holy; without holiness no one will see the Lord.*
> HEBREWS 12:14

Your story

I jump at any opportunity to share about Jesus, but my younger sister was chatting to a boy and said she would pray for his problem, and he freaked out and told her she was brainwashed. Now he keeps going on to her about it, bullying her. My parents and I are trying to support her, but it has affected her.

Freya

Do you sometimes doubt your beliefs? If so, remember what Jesus said:

'Because you have seen me, you have believed; blessed are those who have not seen and yet have believed.'

JOHN 20:29

- Doubts are normal, but don't let them fester. Be honest about them to God and to others. Ask questions, get answers.
- You are *blessed* because you believe the unseen truth of who Jesus is, even though others dispute it. Hold on to that blessing – God's rich love and equipping – and do not let the enemy steal it from you.

Do you feel immature or inexperienced in your understanding of God, and unable to believe he could use you?

- First, your responsibility is simply to believe (John 6:29) and to let the Holy Spirit transform you increasingly into his likeness (2 Corinthians 3:18); out of that, God will work through you all that he has envisioned and equipped you to do.
- Second, be prepared, as well as your circumstances permit, to dig deeper into some answers to those familiar questions of faith.

My friend and I take time out from our larger group of friends if we don't agree with their conversation.

Ella

- Be discerning of the times you need to be the light in the darkness and the times when you need to leave.

Taking it further

Subtle but powerful messages can inform a negative understanding of God and, as a consequence, undermine how we relate to him. For example, living with parents', carers', teachers' or leaders' impossible expectations, repeated broken promises, rejection, disinterest, inconsistency, favouritism, constant distraction, busyness, abuse or abandonment.

We cannot silence these messages overnight, but with time we can eradicate them, as we replace them with truth that frees us from the lies holding us back from our Father, and so bring healing to our broken self-image.

Pause to consider each description of God below.

The Lord:

- does not lie (Numbers 23:19)
- is loving (Psalm 25:10)
- is a father to the fatherless (Psalm 68:5)
- forgives (Psalm 103:3)
- is with you (Psalm 118:6)
- is good (Psalm 145:9)
- is compassionate (Psalm 145:9)
- is faithful to all his promises (Psalm 145:13)
- lifts up all who are bowed down (Psalm 145:14)
- is near (Psalm 145:18)
- heals the broken-hearted (Psalm 147:3)
- strengthens and upholds you (Isaiah 41:10)
- knew you before you were born (Jeremiah 1:5)
- delights in you (Zephaniah 3:17)

- is with you always (Matthew 28:20)
- does not condemn you (John 8:11)
- chose you (John 15:16)
- cares for you (1 Peter 5:7)
- is comforting (2 Corinthians 1:3–4)

Now reflect on the following:

- Which of the descriptions above stand out as truths that you especially need to receive into your heart and soul?
- Speak out and receive these truths in prayer.
- Believe; don't doubt their message.
- Root yourself in who God is, out of which you will grow into the life he created you for.

Pause to respond to God

When you are ready, pray this prayer to commit your response to God:

'Here am I. Send me!'
ISAIAH 6:8

Role models who inspire for reasons other than their appearance

Kate Coleman. She's black, single and in a man's world. A woman who has managed to be influential, who speaks with real authority and writes well. But she's unapologetically a woman, unlike some women in ministry who can be known for being a bit wishy-washy.
Katrina

11

Inflated, deflated or Jesus-motivated

Comparisons and self-image

If you compare yourself to others, you may become vain and bitter; for always there will be greater and lesser persons than yourself.

Max Ehrmann, writer 1872–1945[34]

Our story

The apostle Paul wrote, 'We do not dare to... compare ourselves' (2 Corinthians 10:12), yet we so often do. And because it is so destructive to our self-image, it deserves its own chapter before we move on to Part III.

Here are a few examples of what young women have said about comparison with others.

Comparisons that undermine body image

I feel like I don't look like the 'ideal'. Social media pushes you into that way of thinking... It's the comparing that's the problem.
Chloe

I was once chatting with my then boyfriend about our 'ideal partners' (as in our favourite celebrities). He told me I was great, but if only I were taller and blonde! This had quite an effect on me as it isn't the type of comment you expect from someone who is supposed to be with you for who you are. As a result of this and other things, I ended up having a very low self-image, which really affected my relationship with food. I started to constrict my eating as a way of dealing with my issues. It has definitely had a lasting effect, as I still struggle with trust, although I feel far happier now than I was last year!

Amelia

Comparisons that undermine self-esteem

A big thing that undermines how I feel about myself is comparison. Comparing myself to others is what makes me feel foolish or silly and inadequate.

Lily

Being an identical twin, my sister is my direct comparison. I, she and everyone else have spent a lifetime comparing the two of us, both physically, looking for our differences, and in pretty much every walk of life.

We have had the same upbringing and opportunities, yet she always got better grades in school, no matter how hard I tried! She was chosen over me for the long-jump team in primary school; she is currently engaged and will probably be married before I even have my first boyfriend; and she was recommended to apply for a master's degree, whereas I was recommended to take a year out before applying to get more 'life experience' – things like that.

In a way, I sometimes feel like the rubbishy version of her, like I'm always in her shadow. She would probably disagree, but that's how it sometimes feels.

Molly

Comparisons that undermine self-worth

I find the comparison between what I am taking for exams and what my sisters and friends are taking makes me feel like I'm not as good – that I'm less worthy. I am doing art; they are doing maths and sciences. I am going to art college; they want to be lawyers, doctors and vets. Science seems more academic, and therefore better than to be an artist.

Ella

Even though I get accepted and am therefore good enough for dance productions, I'm always comparing myself with others and it's bad for my self-worth. It seems I compare myself more to others with something I'm good at. And then I think, 'Well if I'm no good at this, then what am I good at?'

Jess

The comparison conundrum

Just because one person your age has achieved certain things doesn't mean that you have to too. Your life is unique. Be proud of that.

Maria Rodrigues, producer and presenter on Premier Christian Radio[35]

Comparing ourselves to others, or listening to others comparing us with somebody else, will make us either proud or jealous, insecure, discontent or depressed, corroding our self-image in the process as we turn our backs on the person God made us to be.

Comparing ourselves to others is immensely destabilising and has the potential over the long term to trigger mental and physical health disorders, because we look in the wrong mirrors to feed our need for approval. We devalue ourselves, or someone else, depending on whether we feel slim or fat, attractive or dull, popular or unwanted, admired or ignored, capable or useless, a success or a failure. Opinions, ideals, fashion and culture are constantly in flux, and so will our self-image be, if it relies on being compared to, and then conformed with, such fluid parameters.

While we can't stop other people making comparisons, we can stop doing it ourselves. We can determine to only compare ourselves with the image of Jesus, and with who God created us to be.

God never intended to clone us; he doesn't want another Anne, Liz or Sophie. Nor does he want us to try to clone ourselves into someone else. He created us as we are for a reason, and he longs that we cherish our uniqueness as much as he does. But our God-given individuality will keep threatening us, if we insist on listening to and looking at the world's mirrors; in turn, we will struggle to become all that God designed us to be.

So let's look at God's mirror again, to help us overcome this problem.

God's mirror image and message

'Be perfect, therefore, as your heavenly Father is perfect.'
MATTHEW 5:48

You're joking, aren't you? No one can do that!

True. And yet this command is vital to renewing a healthy self-image that has been eroded or falsely inflated by being compared with others. When Jesus says, 'Be perfect', it's as if he takes our face in his hands and gently shifts our gaze away from the world's distorted ideals, saying, 'Look! This is what you are aiming for.'

And there he is before us, alive and reflecting back perfect love – strong, pure, beautiful, compassionate, kind and powerful – the image of Father God we were created as his children to grow into and reveal.

Hold on to that image for a moment.

See, no hint of ridicule. No malice. No disappointment or condemnation. All you can see is the bright light of belief in who *he* made you to be and his longing that you will pursue it as your life's purpose.

Your story

Make a careful exploration of who you are and the work you have been given, and then sink yourself into that. Don't be impressed with yourself. Don't compare yourself with others. Each of you must take responsibility for doing the creative best you can with your own life.
GALATIANS 6:4–5 (MSG)

Make a careful exploration of who you are…

- What excites and motivates you about conforming to the image of Jesus?
- How might that challenge other images you try to match up to or even rival?
- Are you willing to let go of whatever holds you back from being transformed into the person God created you to be?

… and the work you have been given…

- Are you doing what God created, equipped and has anointed you to do? Or are you trying to be like someone else – in how they appear, in the fruit they produce or in the social circles they move in?

and then sink yourself into that.

- Are you still trying to conform to too many expectations, or will you dedicate all you have and are to what God has asked you to do?

Don't be impressed with yourself.

- Be encouraged by God's affirmation of who you are and the reassurance he gives you through other people's respect or praise. But do so with your eyes always fixed on Jesus, the only one to aspire to.

Don't compare yourself with others.

- Take this from the apostle Paul:

  We do not dare to classify or compare ourselves with some who commend themselves. When they measure themselves by themselves and compare themselves with themselves, they are not wise. We, however, will not boast beyond proper limits, but will confine our boasting to the sphere of service God himself has assigned to us…
  2 CORINTHIANS 10:12–13

Don't be unwise. Stop comparing yourself to the standards imposed by the world. It is of no godly good to your self-image or to fulfilling your own life's potential.

  … doing the creative best you can with your own life.

- Your upbringing, circumstances, talents, interests, skills, spiritual gifts and experiences, good and bad, are a unique, complex combination that makes up 'you', as exclusively distinctive as your thumbprint from anyone else on earth. You are fit for God's purpose for *you*.
- Find encouragement from others who can empathise with your interests and skills, as well as with the limitations and hardships of your circumstances. But remember: in *every* situation, your best will be different from my best, which will be different from her best.
- Be free to be you. Be true to yourself. Be open to the Spirit. And then soar on the thermals of the divine.

Taking it further

Exam grades are a massive pressure. There is a constant comparison among friends. But someone who gets a C might have worked far harder than the one who got an A*, so the comparison is unfair.
Freya

Let us throw off everything that hinders and the sin that so easily entangles. And let us run with perseverance the race marked out for us, fixing our eyes on Jesus, the pioneer and perfecter of faith. For the joy that was set before him he endured the cross, scorning its shame, and sat down at the right hand of the throne of God. Consider him who endured such opposition from sinners, so that you will not grow weary and lose heart.
HEBREWS 12:1–3

The writer to the Hebrews paints a picture of life as an athletics track, with lanes marked out for each runner. If I keep looking at how you are running in your lane, I will slow my own race down. If I decide to run in your lane, thinking that will make me a better runner, I will be disqualified. In other words, I will fail to fulfil all that God has created me for, if I misdirect my efforts into trying to look or be like someone I'm not.

Instead, I must keep my eyes fixed straight ahead on the tape at the end of the track; I have only myself to compete with, in letting God transform me increasingly into the likeness of his Son.

- What about you? Will you keep your eyes fixed straight ahead? Will you focus on that goal beyond the finishing tape of this life?
- How does this picture help or inspire you?

Not that I have already obtained all this, or have already arrived at my goal, but I press on to take hold of that for which Christ Jesus took hold of me. Brothers and sisters, I do not consider myself yet to have taken hold of it. But one thing I do: forgetting what is behind and straining towards what is ahead, I press on towards the goal to win the prize for which God has called me heavenwards in Christ Jesus.

PHILIPPIANS 3:12–14

- Be encouraged: growing into the image and truth of Jesus is an ongoing process.
- Will you press on towards that goal?

Amen!

Pause to respond to God

Lord, I know I will never be perfect this side of heaven, but thank you for giving me a goal infused with your love. May I never stop short of running straight ahead into your outstretched arms.

I do want to keep my eyes focused on you. Let me never be satisfied to stay as I am when there is so much more of you to grow into, but let me never feel discouraged by comparing myself with others, who are on their own unique journey of life with you.

Jesus, may you alone inspire me to pursue all you made me to be, as I shine your grace on to others.

Role models who inspire for reasons other than their appearance

I admire those who live not for the approval or benefit of others, but on the other hand, not lacking a caring nature or incorporating a selfish stance.

Evie

iii

Moving on

12

A cautionary tale

The potential for self-image issues to harm health

'Do you want to get well?'
JOHN 5:6

My story

20 December 1991, Sydney, Australia

My sandalled feet squelched through the café, while shorts stuck to my tanned wet legs. Sinking into a soft, cushioned seat, I gazed at the menu: hot and cold drinks, sandwiches, panini, baked potatoes, a list of sumptuous fillings and tantalising home-baked cakes.

I felt a dilemma brewing; that's what I called those moments of anxious indecision. It was a battle between calories and control, between hunger and the fear of getting fat – a battle rampaging relentlessly through my head.

The previous week, I had treated myself to a slice of carrot cake, devouring it in a few blissful moments. But I had then fought the guilt and rage with myself for days, going without dinner that night and taking a long walk to burn off the evidence instead.

The waitress arrived, forcing me out of my dilemma to choose this week's treat. A pot of tea *with* milk.

By the third cup my hunger had subsided. I leaned back, closed my eyes and embraced warmth.

Your body is a temple.

Startled, I sat bolt upright. The words had emerged from an unseen realm, penetrating my deepest being. My body is a temple? Somehow the phrase was familiar, but surely not...

I rummaged in my rucksack for my pocket Bible, and by some miracle of grace turned straight to the page containing the following:

> *Do you not know that your bodies are temples of the Holy Spirit...*
> *Therefore honour God with your bodies.*
> 1 CORINTHIANS 6:19–20

I glanced down at the ripple of protruding bones fanning out across my chest.

'But how? How do I escape this terror?' I whispered.

July 1992, Guernsey

I knew I had been putting on weight – I could feel the sickening sensation on my waistline – but there hadn't been any scales to check. So, on the day I returned from my travel adventures, I locked the bathroom door, dreading what I might read when I weighed myself.

Five-and-a-half stone.

I stared in disbelief, wondering how low my weight had actually dropped before my healing began with that moment of conviction in the Sydney cafe to seek help for anorexia.

The physical struggle continued for a few more years as I learned to accept my increasing size. The emotional and psychological battle, however, was not helped when my weight ballooned temporarily, as my once-starved body continued in survival mode, storing rather than burning up the new and ample supply of fuel it was now receiving. But when my weight settled to a healthy level for a woman of my height and frame, I remember telling my sister that I didn't think I would ever be healed of the mental conflict.

I was wrong.

As I kept steeping myself in God's love and engaging with his truth, I did find complete freedom and healing. So I offer that hope to any of you who are still in the thick of the fight.

Sadly, however, this isn't everyone's story; many have died from such issues. Addiction and mental disorders are complex illnesses, and it would be wrong to suggest they are purely down to low self-image. That said, low self-image was *one* of the triggers for my problems, and it also may have been for my brother, who tragically died, aged 43, from the long-term effects of alcoholism.

A factor that may have contributed to his addiction was his height, or lack of it. As a child, he was always the shortest in his class, and as an adult, he barely reached 5 ft, so you can imagine the bullying and the endless jokes that were made at his expense, and the potential these had, despite his skills and successful career as a chef, to fuel a sense of inadequacy as a man.

An ongoing problem

9 in 10 women stop themselves from eating or otherwise put their health at risk (e.g. avoid going to the doctor) when they don't feel good about themselves.[36]

Reseach books and reports suggest a variety of reasons for the rise of eating disorders, drug and alcohol addiction, self-harm, depression and promiscuity, which include the following:

- long-term low self-esteem
- poor body image
- lack of self-worth
- self-hatred
- inner conflict or emptiness
- painful experiences
- absence of love and affection
- undue influence of media portrayals of success or the 'ideal' body

Many of us have days when we suffer a low mood, but allowing negative thoughts to keep rumbling around our heads permits them to grow and, in time, start taking control.

I've met women who have lived with anorexia for 40 years. Physically, they have survived; but much of their potential lies buried beneath emotional insecurity, manipulative behaviour, self-imposed destructive labels and broken relationships. I've met others whose flourishing careers have been snuffed out after persistent self-harming landed them in hospital long-term. And I've sat with souls imprisoned in darkness, despairing of finding a way out.

That may be the extreme, but someone doesn't have to end up with a clinically confirmed illness to suffer repercussions from low self-image. This chapter has a message for us all: a warning of what happens if we continue to let the world's mirrors dictate our priorities, worth and purpose.

Low mood, anxiety, withdrawal from social circles or usual activities, disillusionment, hopelessness, insecurity and an undermining of confidence and worth have all been mentioned in response to my self-image questionnaire. It suggests that many of us struggle with negative thoughts and their impact on our self-esteem or self-worth.

Self-image issues are not just girlish fads; they can affect us physically, emotionally, mentally and spiritually. Overcoming them isn't easy. Choices have to be made and proactive steps taken, and I know from experience how frightening that can feel. For although our negative issue may not be good for us, it can, paradoxically, offer a place of security – of familiarity, safety and self-acceptance.

When Jesus told the paralysed man to pick up his mat and walk (John 5:8), the man must have felt that fear too: 'What if it hurts? What if what they say about Jesus isn't true? What if I fall over and people laugh? What if I disappoint my friends? What will I do with my life if I am no longer cared for by others?'

The man had to take a step of faith – just one – in order to break through the fear that could have barred his way to healing. And *then* he was miraculously healed.

'Do you want to get well?' Jesus asked the invalid of 38 years lying by the Pool of Bethesda (John 5:1–6). He asked me that question too, and I was terrified! To say 'yes' meant to put on weight and to potentially lose the sense of (false) self-esteem and (false) self-worth I had built from controlling my intake of food.

Jesus asks you today, 'Do you want to be rid of the pressure to conform, look a certain way, attain an unrealistic benchmark of success, be like a certain person?'

If so, first identify your snare – the issue that 'paralyses' you or the specific mirror image or message that stops you experiencing the fullness of God's love and promises and pursuing your God-given potential. Then take the first step towards walking away.

And remember – all he asks is that you take one step at a time. Just one. Then another…

Your story

> *Do you not know that your bodies are temples of the Holy Spirit,*
> *who is in you, whom you have received from God? You are not*
> *your own; you were bought at a price. Therefore honour God with*
> *your bodies.*
> 1 CORINTHIANS 6:19–20

Mental health is only one thing affected by low self-image. If we are relentlessly self-critical, labelling ourselves with demeaning names, hating our bodies, telling ourselves that no one is interested in what we have to say, or shaming our mistakes and failures, our bodies will respond to the internal stress by releasing chemicals that, in turn, lower immunity. So let's be sure to give our awesome bodies the TLC they deserve, the attention God designed them to be given.

Are you allowing yourself enough hours to sleep?

Sleep is vital for overall health and well-being (Psalm 127:2). Recommendations range from seven to nine hours per day for those aged 18 to 64, or eight to ten hours for 14–17-year-olds. I admit this may be impossible for young mums or, for example, parents of disabled children. But is it really impossible for you?

Do you generally eat a nutritious, healthy diet?

You really *are* what you eat! And I hope that, from reading this book, you believe you're worth taking good care of. What kinds of 'bricks and mortar' are you using to build and maintain God's holy temple, your body?

Low levels of vitamins, minerals, omega-3 and water, fluctuations in blood sugar, or food allergies and sensitivities can lower mood, create feelings of sluggishness or depression, generate anxiety, interfere with concentration and mimic various mental-health issues.

Check out 'Food and Mood' on the Mind website (www.mind.org.uk) for further tips on what to eat.

Are you getting enough exercise?

As well as being beneficial to your heart, bones, muscles and so on, exercise releases chemicals that lift your mood, increase your energy, warm you up when it's cold and help you sleep.

Choose something you enjoy. I've never been a runner – my knees won't even let me now – and I've never liked the loud sweaty confines of a gym. But I love to walk – fast!

What would inspire you to get up and raise your heartbeat, pound your limbs and limber up for half an hour, five days a week? Powering up and down a swimming pool, adding on extra lengths as the weeks pass by? Pumping iron in the gym with a friend? Joining a local sports club to play tennis, hockey, netball or to go jogging? Dancing to a fitness DVD in the privacy of your home? Joining an exercise class with your friends? We're certainly not short of options.

Do you have a day off work every week?

God's instruction to rest is a gift (Exodus 20:9–10). Rejecting it suggests that we are striving to achieve or to build our worth and significance independently of him, or that we are refusing to trust he knows best. Not taking a day off is also a direct, wilful act of disobedience to the fourth commandment.

What really helps you relax? What energises you? A day of rest is not the time to be catching up with tasks that stress or irritate you. And remember: rest is to help you focus on God, as well as to restore your well-being. Try to be more aware of him, whatever you choose to do. If possible, use some of the time to be present with him in a verse or short passage of scripture. Immerse yourself in it – in him.

What do you do to have fun?

Recent research suggests that doing something you enjoy can also lead to improved psychological and physical well-being. Taking a breather from routine demands, whether having coffee with friends, enjoying the great outdoors, chilling out to music or whatever else gives you pleasure, can be beneficial to coping and restoration, especially when stressed.

Jesus often accepted invitations to dinner and took time out with his best friends. He changed water into wedding wine and would surely have joked, laughed, sung and danced in traditional Jewish style. Jesus made time to enjoy himself while still focused on his Father's presence, intent on revealing him to those he was with. And that can be true for us too.

Do you have someone you can trust to share with and pray confidentially about your worries and insecurities?

Not having someone to confide in when dealing with painful, troubling or difficult situations leads to self-blame, misunderstandings and buried emotions, all of which erode self-esteem and self-worth.

Remember: to have a friend and confidant means to *be* one too. Can you be trusted with your friend's privacy as much as you want to trust them with yours? Try to keep in touch with them as much as you hope they will keep in touch with you. A text, a call, a coffee and chat – it doesn't need to take much, but it is tremendously rewarding (Proverbs 17:17; 18:24; 27:6, 10).

Taking it further

As I wrote in the introduction, if you already suffer mentally or physically, then please do consult your GP, ask to see a specialised counsellor or join a support group – or just start by talking to a trusted friend. But please do not do nothing.

Other potential contacts

www.mind.org.uk
www.livingout.org
www.selfharm.org.uk
www. youngminds.co.uk
www. overcomedepression.co.uk
www.eatingdisordersanonymous.org
www.alcoholics-anonymous.co.uk
www.nanj.org (Narcotics Anonymous)
www. helenawilkinson.co.uk (for Christian help with eating disorders
and related issues)

Pause to respond to God

Set me free from my prison, that I may praise your name.
PSALM 142:7

• Perhaps you long to be healed, but are terrified at the prospect. Keep praying this prayer to help you make that first step.

Or consider your personal response to 1 Corinthians 6:19–20.

• What does this say to you about the way you treat your body, the home of God's Spirit in you?
• Talk to God about it now.

Role models who inspire for reasons other than their appearance

Here is the story behind one of my own role models.

I can recall that night so clearly, a year or two before I went travelling. The lights were dim as I snuggled beneath my duvet, some way through reading Puppet on a String, *the autobiography of Helena Wilkinson, who had suffered with anorexia nervosa.*

Mum had bought it for me, saying, 'I thought you might enjoy this. Perhaps find it interesting.'

I've always liked biographies, so thinking nothing more of it I had started to read. But that night, my heart was caught by Helena's description of how she had felt. And in that instant I knew – I was anorexic.

Until then, the idea hadn't crossed my mind, though it had obviously crossed my mum's! I felt an odd relief at the revelation, but at the same time sheer dread.

Helena Wilkinson – a woman who courageously shared her story, who is a qualified counsellor and an equine-assisted psychotherapy practitioner, and who lives to bring hope and healing to others with eating disorders and related issues – was and is my role model.

Although the 'how' eluded me and the idea terrified me, deep within I desperately wanted the freedom that she had.

13

Learning to be content

Letting go of self-image issues and holding tight to God

Don't let us love the road rather than the land to which it leads, lest we lose our homeland altogether.

St Columbanus, c.543–615

My story

19 June 1992, a peasant farmstead in Maharashtra, India

After two months in the mission field, I had grown accustomed to my bed – a thin mat on a tiled floor. But I still woke before 5.00 am and slipped out of the tiny room quietly so as not to disturb the four other occupants.

Bucket in hand, I headed for the household's only water tap in the hope of refilling the empty barrels. The supply wasn't turned on every day, and even if it was, it was only available for at most one hour.

I smiled, and silently wished myself a happy birthday.

19 June 1993, Paris, France

It had been an early start, but by late morning two uniformed doormen had greeted me with 'Bonjour, Mademoiselle,' and swung wide the grand entrance doors.

I stepped out of the midsummer heat into air-conditioned luxury and drank in the surroundings: a vast marble floor, a polished brass reception counter, gold-embroidered lounge chairs, plush Persian rugs and swathes of cream voile framing floor-to-ceiling windows that gazed out on a yellow-canopied courtyard.

'Happy birthday!' my soon-to-be fiancé whispered into my ear, before disappearing to register our arrival.

I couldn't move. I was overwhelmed by the opulent surroundings, which jarred with the vivid memory of the desperate poverty where I had been this time the previous year. Guilt seeped stealthily through my soul as I began a silent prayer. But guilt is not the same as conviction, and God's Spirit gently spoke his word to my heart:

> *I know what it is to be in need, and I know what it is to have plenty. I have learned the secret of being content in any and every situation…*
> PHILIPPIANS 4:12

The path to contentment with ourselves and with life

Contentment: mental or emotional satisfaction with things as they are; peace of mind; accepting one's situation or life with satisfaction and equanimity (that is, calmness of mind or temper; composure).[37]

As I mentioned in the introduction, learning how to be content is essential to overcoming issues of low self-image. This involves letting go of unrealistic expectations; being at peace with who God made us to be; appreciating and caring for our God-designed body; and living in and out of the truth of God's love rather than the world's shifting parameters of acceptance.

Developing a healthy, godly self-image is not the same as being surrounded by constant praise, continually hearing the message that we are wonderful or the best, that we can achieve anything we want and that our dreams are always in reach.

Nor is it to live with the clouded perception that we can avoid hard work or difficulty.

We may not achieve every dream we once cherished, but we will learn to let go of them as we open our hearts to God's vision for life. We may not be as 'successful' as we, or our parents or teachers, once hoped we would be, but we will be at peace with pursuing a life that influences people for Jesus. We may not be as 'beautiful' as models on the catwalk or images on social media, but we will be inspired to reflect the nature of Jesus, as we let his Spirit transform us increasingly into his image. We may not have everything we want, but we will learn to be appreciative and satisfied when we have what we need. There may come a time when we have to let go and let others take over a role or responsibility we once held, but we will feel secure in our ongoing path that follows in God's footsteps. Promotion might offer new opportunities, but remaining where we are will not undermine our worth.

We will have learned to be content in God's will, whatever that may be.

And when crying tears of hardship and pain, we will learn to immerse ourselves in God's peace, resting in the comfort of his love, and finding his strength to cope with each day as we walk it, hand in hand with Jesus.

So how do we continue to build on our response to this book's teaching, and learn how to experience the contentment in God that the apostle Paul talks about in his letter to the Philippians?

Adopting the right perspective on life

The Spirit of God whets our appetite by giving us a taste of what's ahead. He puts a little of heaven in our hearts so that we'll never settle for less.
2 CORINTHIANS 5:5 (MSG)

Living in this visible, tangible world can so easily distract us from the invisible reality of God and the heavenly realm. Let's face it, if we could physically see God with us 24/7, I bet we would do a lot of things very differently, and I'm sure we would feel differently about ourselves too. But nurturing an awareness of God with us, as well as our ultimate destination in life, keeps us from entrenching ourselves in a world of fleeting, and sometimes meaningless, goals.

The apostle Paul writes:

Set your minds on things above, not on earthly things.
COLOSSIANS 3:2

What we set our minds on will ultimately define us. If we remain immersed in our culture, its mirror images and messages will continue to inform our thinking and priorities and how we feel. Of course, our culture is the context in which we live, serve and work, but that doesn't imply that our thoughts and hearts have to be confined to its boundaries.

Setting our minds on things above does not mean jacking in our education, job, relationships or responsibilities; it means seeing them from God's perspective. It's about setting our minds on how Jesus wants to be involved in our day, and how our activity can influence others for God's kingdom. And, of course, it means continually nurturing our focus on our first love.

The greater our devotion to Jesus as Lord in our hearts and minds, the more tightly we will hold to his values and purpose, rather than the ties and pulls of the world.

> *So we fix our eyes not on what is seen, but on what is unseen, since what is seen is temporary, but what is unseen is eternal.*
> 2 CORINTHIANS 4:18

Your story

Reflect on the things you do through your day.

- What motivates or drives you to do what you do '*to be loved*'?
- Consider what you might do differently or not at all '*because*' you are loved?
- Try adopting that new perspective from now on.

Zena suffered with bulimia. She says that although she did feel counselling could help, she needed something deeper, and it was her faith in Jesus that proved to be the key to her initial recovery and to sustaining it.

> *Lack of belief in yourself, that's a lot of it. When I realised I was on earth for a reason, that I was a special individual, life began to make sense. That has been really powerful to me. I couldn't have done it by myself.*
> Zena

- You are part of God's unfolding story. Your gifts and talents can be used to impact and transform lives and situations. Do you believe in the 'you' God created you to be?

Bring to mind refugee women fleeing violent, oppressive regimes, waiting at borders for just one person to reach out to them with kindness and care; kidnapped young women imprisoned in the sex trade, violated and despairing of finding a way to escape; and girls being forced to endure FGM,[38] suffering unthinkable pain and trauma.

- Looking outside ourselves helps nurture God's perspective on a broken world, not to depress us or condemn us about the life we enjoy, but to cultivate God's compassion in our hearts and appreciation for the life we have, and to prepare us for how he might rouse us to pray for and practically help others.
- Perhaps a godly perspective is something you feel you need to ask him for now.

I get very anxious and it becomes a cycle of anxiety. I need to change my perspective to get out of the cycle. Negative thoughts can isolate me; they stop me from being sociable or doing anything. It spirals. I retreat into myself and won't connect with people, though I know that connecting would help! It's a dark cloud.

Yasmin

I asked Yasmin how she got herself out of that. She replied:

I pray. When I am in the car with loud praise music, I can shout at God, and it helps! But it especially helps to write out Bible verses and stick them on my noticeboard. It regrounds me, and I don't have to worry. My husband helps, as he jokes about stuff I've taken too seriously, and gives me a better perspective.

How might being real with God help shift your focus and restore a better perspective?

- Where would be a good place for you to place Bible verses? I've had two on my laptop's screen background recently, to keep my perspective on trusting God to help me write this book!

Taking it further

God encourages us to be thankful, because it shifts our perspective back on to our source of life, our provider, our comforter, and his presence with us through every day (e.g. Psalm 118:1; 1 Thessalonians 5:18).

Moreover, studies suggest that nurturing an attitude of thankfulness increases our sense of well-being and can help us overcome low mood.

If you recognise this is something you need to develop, here are some suggestions to start with.

Practise being grateful

Thank God daily for your home, food, fresh water, clothing and medical provision. Thank him for the love of family or friends, your education, resources, opportunities or your work. It will take your focus away from what you haven't got – be that in physical appearance, health or 'success' – and on to the valuable things that you do have. Perhaps you could keep a notebook of what you are thankful for, a tangible list you can turn to if you feel low or distracted by the world.

Keep thanking God for his love for you

I'm not suggesting a daily rote prayer, such as 'Thank you for your love, Lord,' but a pause to receive God's love for you, to be present in, to dwell in and to immerse yourself in that love, and in turn to grow in genuine gratitude for him. Doing this will root your soul ever deeper in his love, which is the source of contentment and a healthy self-esteem and self-worth.

Be thankful, even when life is dull or bleak

When we are feeling bored, fed up or despondent, our attention can become too focused on ourselves. But looking out for things that you are still grateful for will bring light into the darkness. Be thankful for:

- your clothes in the mundane routine of washing and drying them (or ironing and putting them away if you do that; I didn't like to assume!)
- the home that you need to clean
- the opportunity to study even though friends are socialising
- the rain that is watering essential crops but messing up your hair
- the money to buy food as you haul heavy bags up flights of stairs.

Start a thankfulness journal

Aim to write down one thing every day you are grateful for this week, and perhaps next week aim for three. You might also like to read *One Thousand Gifts* by Ann Voskamp, an illuminating, beautifully written story of gratitude.[39]

Pause to respond to God

When you are struggling to silence the bombardment of the world's mirror images and messages, pray:

> *One thing I ask from the Lord, this only do I seek: that I may dwell in the house of the Lord all the days of my life, to gaze on the beauty of the Lord and to seek him in his temple.*
> PSALM 27:4

- Let this prayer remind you of the true source of your worth and to dwell on – to focus on and be aware of – Jesus with you.

When problems, confusion and discouragement threaten your sense of well-being, respond to the advice to 'Be still,' and in that stillness 'know that [he is] God' (Psalm 46:10).

- Just as Jesus commanded the storm-swept Sea of Galilee to be still, choose to still your thoughts, opinions and fears.
- And then *know* – believe and focus on – God's love and promises *with* you.

Remind yourself, often, that your life's path is ultimately heading to heaven.

- Reflect on passages such as John 14:1–4; Revelation 7:11–12, 16–17; 21:1–4, 16–27.
- Renew a worshipping focus on your eternal home by immersing your heart's response in relevant songs. Look on YouTube for songs to inspire your worship, perhaps starting with 'There is a Higher Throne' by Keith Getty and Kristyn Lennox Getty.

Role models who inspire for reasons other than their appearance

Those women who are positive people, who live with their glass half full and are content with their own company.
Evie

14

Beyond this book

Putting it into practice

Motivation is what gets you started. Habit is what keeps you going.

Jim Ryan, athlete

My story

Whatever you have learned or received or heard from me, or seen in me – put it into practice. And the God of peace will be with you.
PHILIPPIANS 4:9

My story is mine, so I don't expect you to relate to everything I have shared, or to adopt everything I've suggested. But I was challenged to be honest with you about my vulnerabilities, in the hope that there would be something, somewhere, for you to connect with.

My question now is: what has God spoken to *you* through this book? What has the Holy Spirit inspired deep within your heart? What truth do you need to receive, learn and respond to, in thought and action?

It will take time for God's truth to replace the distorted images and messages that have undermined your self-image – time for you to read, hear, believe and respond in faith, and to let it carve out new ways of thinking and being within your soul.

Carving new grooves and ruts

Negative thinking affects the way I eat and makes me feel less confident.
Amelia

Negative thinking has the ability to make me hesitate and doubt myself. It can slow me down from stepping out of comfort zones.
Lily

I try to be optimistic where possible and stay away from negative thoughts, but when they do hit, I guess they get me down quite a lot and make me feel vulnerable and timid. Not worthless as such, but worth less.
Molly

When a car repeatedly travels the same way down a country track, it begins to carve out grooves in the earth. In time, deep ruts appear, guiding the wheels down the usual route unless someone yanks the steering wheel to launch the car out of the ruts on to a new course.

Similarly, cultural mirror images and messages form grooves, then ruts, in our thinking and response. The longer we let their opinions dictate our thought patterns, the deeper the ruts and the less resistant we become to the distortions undermining our well-being – to the point that we might barely even realise they are there.

But the apostle Paul teaches us to 'take captive every thought to make it obedient to Christ' (2 Corinthians 10:5). This means addressing every negative thought inspired by cultural mirrors, then surrendering it to the truth that we see in and hear from God, 'fitting every loose thought and emotion and impulse into the structure of life shaped by Christ' (*The Message*).

We won't get fitter by reading a book on diet or exercise unless we also work out and eat the right food. Likewise, merely reading this book, or any self-image manual, will not remove our issues unless we put into practice what we have learned.

So we need to choose to either continue with negative thoughts or take them captive and carve out new ruts! We need to be aware of the subtle messages and choose daily to 'yank the steering wheel', allowing God's word to carve new truths through our mind, heart and soul.

That is why memorising scripture is key to feeding our roots in who we are in God. As we drive those words over and over down the tracks of our mind and heart, their truth will become our natural pattern of thinking.

God's word is 'living'. When we let it be formed within us, it is powerful in its effect on transforming our old responses, while renewing our inward being with truth protects us from ongoing pressure to conform to the expectations of our culture and world (Romans 12:2).

Your story

*Someone told [Jesus], 'Your mother and brothers are standing outside, wanting to see you.' He replied, 'My mother and brothers are those who hear God's word and **put it into practice**.'*
LUKE 8:20–21 (MY BOLD)

What has especially spoken to you or challenged you in this book?

- What are you looking at and listening to that has more impact and influence on you than God's truth? Identify the specific images and messages undermining who you are. This will help you face them, deal with them and move on.
- What triggers those messages? Certain situations, perhaps, that create uncertainty about who God made you to be? A particular

social media feed that constantly makes you feel bad? A person who leaves you feeling inadequate in some kind of way?

- Avoiding these situations, feeds or people may not be the answer, but recognising them as triggers will remind you to be armed with God's truth in advance of the next encounter.
- Do you need to take more time in God's word? Do you need to read more widely, and not just your favourite passages?
- Do you need to stop talking negatively to yourself, putting yourself down or hiding behind others because you don't believe you have anything of worth to say or offer? Hear it when you say it, forgive yourself, speak truth to yourself and determine not to say it again.
- Do you need to gain a new perspective on life – on God's definition of purpose, meaning and success?
- Do you need to get further medical help, to accompany your deepening relationship with God?
- Do you need to take time out from social media more often?
- Do you have to choose to stop comparing yourself to your sibling, friends, adverts or online images?
- Do you just need to make a daily choice, hourly even, to keep turning your face to look in the mirror reflecting back Jesus – the reality of his presence, the beauty of his character, the truth of his messages to your soul?

A question, based on Joshua 24:15:

If you feel that being loved by God is not enough to satisfy you, if you feel that loving him can sit way down on your priority list, if you think that serving him is pointless and won't achieve what you or other people want you to achieve, then make a choice. Today. Now. Choose for yourself to whom or what you will give your attention, focus, money, study, talent, time and devotion; whose opinions and expectations will dictate your life; whose beauty you will aspire to. As for me, I will love and serve Jesus.

This book is approaching its end, but your life continues beyond its pages. Consider the proactive suggestions below. Which ones might you need to keep repeating, after our brief journey together fades from the forefront of your mind?

- Choose to adopt your identity in Christ from now on.
- Believe in your worth to God for who you are, and not for what you do.
- Accept the part you were chosen to play in his will.
- Reach out for and use his spiritual riches to equip you.
- Honour the image and name of your Father that is intrinsic to who you are.
- Live in and out of his unending, unconditional, higher than high, wider than wide, deeper than deep love for you.
- Stop using the words 'ought' and 'should'.
- Ditch the negative labels you have been calling yourself.
- Believe your opinions are worth being heard.
- Be secure enough in God to admit when you are wrong.
- Seek to be filled with enough of God's grace and love to know when to keep silent.
- Love others with integrity and not to gain their approval or praise.

Put a note somewhere you can see it, to remind you of the choices and actions you need to keep on making beyond this book.

Taking it further

A friend to share life with and be accountable to

I have been meeting with young people in schools to listen to their voices about what matters to them and how we can challenge the perception of value being associated with body image. I long for every young person to discover their worth as a unique individual created in the image of God and to find happiness as they go on becoming who they have been created to be.

Rt Revd Rachel Treweek, Bishop of Gloucester[40]

You may not have the lovely bishop knocking on your door, but is there someone you could approach to walk your journey with you? Someone you could share your worries and insecurities with, someone to hold you accountable for your lifestyle choices, someone to pray with and for you?

Developing a godly self-image is not just concerned with feeling better about ourselves; it is respecting and appreciating who God made us to be, and honouring him with our bodies, behaviour, talents, time and resources. It dovetails with self-discipline, patience and personal and spiritual growth, and with accepting what God has enabled us to do – as well as what he has not! And sometimes that needs a trusted, prayerful, godly friend to help us see life from God's perspective.

A role model to inspire you

Jesus gives the ultimate example of a life to look to for inspiration, but there is nothing wrong with having a female role model – a woman we admire for reasons other than her appearance or 'success', and from whom we can learn.

They are not saints or goddesses and they do make mistakes, so let's not idolise them, or become so focused on one woman that we are blinded to the treasure and inspiration in someone else. And remember, the purpose of a role model is not to make us compare ourselves with them, but for us to be inspired by them.

I can think of a handful of women in who I see the authentic reflection of Jesus – self-assurance fed from his love; integrity of faith lived out in everyday life; strength to endure extreme difficulties; passion to reach out for the life God has called them to; and a heart that beats to God's gargantuan heart for the poor, oppressed and unsaved.

We can learn from women who have learned from their own mistakes, and are humble enough to share how. We can learn from women who are generous with themselves, who will never put others down no matter how they are treated, and whose own self-image is not hampered by the success, beauty, popularity or spiritual gifting of anyone else in the room.

They are women who are deeply secure in who God made them to be and are content in him, whatever their stage of life. They have simply learned to put into practice what we may still be learning today, and when we see the awesome effect it has had in and through their lives, it is hugely inspiring to want to live out what we have learned too.

Pause to respond to God

Take your worship – your surrendered, devoted life of love and witness – beyond the confines of your prayer time, small group or Sunday meeting. Worship Jesus with your life in every moment of each day, always looking up for a glimpse of his presence, to shift your focus away from the distorted mirrors lining the way.

As you do, I will 'keep asking that the God of our Lord Jesus Christ, the glorious Father, may give you the Spirit of wisdom and revelation, so that you may know him better. I pray that the eyes of your heart may be enlightened in order that you may know the hope to which he has called you, the riches of his glorious inheritance in his holy people, and his incomparably great power for us who believe' (Ephesians 1:17–19).

Role models who inspire for reasons other than their appearance

A lady at church: she's like my mother. We have a Ruth-and-Naomi relationship. What influences me is her character; she is so wise, patient and understanding. She has the ability to let me see the bigger picture in different situations. She is also a woman of prayer and intercession, and when I see her passion for prayer and hear of all the testimonies she has, it really influences me and encourages me to be content in how my Father has made me and to walk in the calling he has placed on my life.

Lily

Notes

1   Cognitive behavioural therapy is a form of talking treatment by which patients are taught to recognise how their thought patterns, beliefs and attitudes are affecting their behaviour. When successful, it enables them to manage their problems by making helpful alterations to the way they think and therefore behave.

2   Dove Self-Esteem Project, 2013, www.selfesteem.dove.us/Articles/Written/What_is_body_confidence.aspx.

3   The pseudonyms bear no resemblance to any of the names of respondents that I was made aware of from discussion groups or email responses. I have no idea who posted the anonymous replies, however, so I apologise if you read yourself quoted with a pseudonym that bears resemblance to your name. But please don't worry; after all, only you will know.

4   Chris Williams, *I'm Not Good Enough*, Living Life to the Full series (Five Areas Resources, 2008), p. 3.

5   The YWAM discipleship-training course included a two-month mission trip to India.

6   Richard J. Foster, *Celebration of Discipline* (Hodder & Stoughton, 1978), p. 63.

7   Brother Andrew, *One Week Walking with Our Persecuted Brothers and Sisters* (Open Doors Booklet, 2013), Day 7.

8   Jeremiah J. Johnston, *Unanswered* (Whitaker House, 2015), p. 162.

9   Based on an original quote from Xun Kuang, a Confucian philosopher, 312–230BC.

10 See, for example, www.premierdigital.org.uk/Resources/Social-Media/Why-you-should-think-twice-before-ditching-your-paper-Bible-in-favour-of-an-App and www.bbc.com/future/story/20170222-how-smartphones-and-social-media-are-changing-religion.

11 *The Dove Global Beauty and Confidence Report* (Dove, 2016), Foreword, p. 1.

12 *The Dove Global Beauty and Confidence Report*, infographic.

13 Government Equalities Office, *Body Confidence Campaign: Progress*

report (2015), pp. 5, 7. Available at www.gov.uk/government/
publications/body-confidence-progress-report-2015.

14   Government Equalities Office, *Body Confidence Campaign*, p. 4.

15   Youth Work Resource, 'the mirrors' mp3 track, www.
youthworkresource.com/wp-content/uploads/2011/06/mirrors_
script.mp3. The background track is 'Shared Loneliness' by Mind
Things.

16   Lupita Nyong'o, award acceptance speech at the 2014 Black Women
in Hollywood Luncheon.

17   *Girls' Wellbeing Explored: Understanding pressures and resilience*
(Girlguiding, 2016), p. 15. Available at www.girlguiding.org.uk/
globalassets/docs-and-resources/research-and-campaigns/girls-
wellbeing-explored-think-resilient-report.pdf.

18   For example, Revelation 4:2–6; 21:1–4, 16–27.

19   Hilary McDowell, *Some Day I'm Going to Fly* (Triangle SPCK, 1995),
p. 2.

20   Laura Thomas, 'A stroke freed me to redefine beauty', *Christianity
Today*, 19 February 2017, www.christianitytoday.com/women/2017/
february/stroke-freed-me-from-fleeting-beauty.html. See also
Katherine's own website at www.hopeheals.com.

21   McDowell, *Some Day I'm Going to Fly*, pp. 2–3, 74–75.

22   McDowell, *Some Day I'm Going to Fly*, pp. 76–77.

23   National Archives for the UK Office for National Statistics, using data
from the Annual Population Survey collected between April 2011 and
March 2012. Personal well-being statistics between October 2015
and September 2016 continued to reflect this fact.

24   Thomas, 'A stroke freed me to redefine beauty'.

25   @davewillis Twitter post, 24 August 2014, https://twitter.com/
davewillis/status/503639941822550016.

26   *The Dove Global Beauty and Confidence Report*, p. 21.

27   Royal Society for Public Health (RSPH) and Young Health Movement,
*#StatusOfMind: Social media and young people's mental health and
wellbeing*, 19 May 2017, pp. 3, 13–16, www.rsph.org.uk/our-work/
policy/social-media-and-young-people-s-mental-health-and-
wellbeing.html.

28   *The Changing Face of Beauty: 2004 to 2024*, p. 5, commissioned by
Dove, collated by Canvas8.

29   Further information and updates on the Bishop of Gloucester's
#liedentity campaign page can be found at www.gloucester.anglican.
org/parish-resources/communications/liedentity.

30   Two Listeners, *God Calling*, edited by A.J. Russell (Arthur James, 1953), p. 237.

31   *The Dove Global Beauty and Confidence Report*, infographic.

32   Maria Rodrigues, @WomaninLondon Twitter post, 11 January 2017, https://twitter.com/WomaninLondon/status/819173551391514624.

33   Jo Griffin, *The Lonely Society* (Mental Health Foundation, 2010).

34   From his prose poem 'Desiderata' (1927). Available at http://mwkworks.com/desiderata.html.

35   Maria Rodrigues, @WomaninLondon Twitter post, 28 December 2016, https://twitter.com/WomaninLondon/status/814214833965068288.

36   *The Dove Global Beauty and Confidence Report*, infographic.

37   Definition taken from *Collins English Dictionary*, 1979.

38   Female genital mutilation: the practice of cutting or removing some or all of the external female genitalia, in order to control a woman's sexuality.

39   Ann Voskamp, *One Thousand Gifts* (Zondervan, 2010).

40   Further information and updates on the Bishop of Gloucester's #liedentity campaign page can be found at www.gloucester.anglican.org/parish-resources/communications/liedentity.